A Study after 1900

History for NI Key Stage 3

A Study after 1900

- **Sheelagh Dean**   - **Vivien Kelly**   - **Julie Taggart**

HODDER
EDUCATION
AN HACHETTE UK COMPANY

Photo credits and acknowledgements appear on p. 108

Although every effort has been made to ensure that website addresses are correct at time of going to press, Hodder Education cannot be held responsible for the content of any website mentioned in this book. It is sometimes possible to find a relocated web page by typing in the address of the home page for a website in the URL window of your browser.

Hachette UK's policy is to use papers that are natural, renewable and recyclable products and made from wood grown in sustainable forests. The logging and manufacturing processes are expected to conform to the environmental regulations of the country of origin.

Orders: please contact Bookpoint Ltd, 130 Milton Park, Abingdon, Oxon OX14 4SB. Telephone: (44) 01235 827720. Fax: (44) 01235 400454. Lines are open 9.00–5.00, Monday to Saturday, with a 24-hour message answering service. Visit our website at www.hoddereducation.co.uk

© **Sheelagh Dean, Vivien Kelly, Julie Taggart 2009**
First published in 2009 by
Hodder Education,
An Hachette UK Company
338 Euston Road
London NW1 3BH

Impression number   7
Year   2014

Cover photo © Tony Pleavin/Alamy
Illustrations by Barking Dog/Tony Randall
Typeset in Imperial 10.5pt by Fakenham Prepress Solutions, Fakenham, Norfolk, NR21 8NN
Printed in Dubai

A catalogue record for this title is available from the British Library

ISBN: 978 0340 81482 6

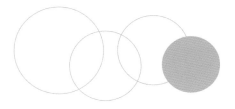

Contents

Your pathway through this book

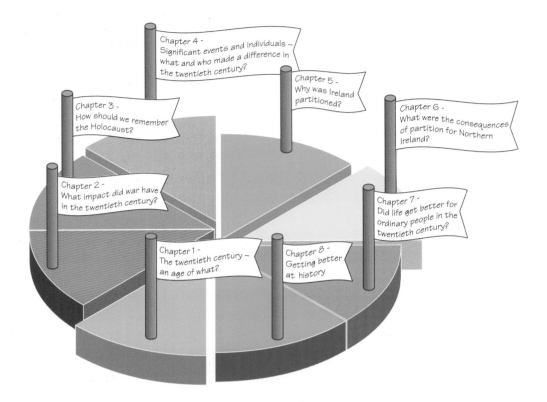

Chapter 4 -
Significant events and individuals – what and who made a difference in the twentieth century?

Chapter 5 -
Why was Ireland partitioned?

Chapter 3 -
How should we remember the Holocaust?

Chapter 6 -
What were the consequences of partition for Northern Ireland?

Chapter 2 -
What impact did war have in the twentieth century?

Chapter 7 -
Did life get better for ordinary people in the twentieth century?

Chapter 1 -
The twentieth century – an age of what?

Chapter 8 -
Getting better at history

As you make your way through this book, you will start to develop the skills you need to be good at and enjoy history. The eight flagposts above show the chapter titles in the book, each of which asks a big question.

SKILLS AND CAPABILITIES

In Chapters 1–7 you will find:

- **Learning Intentions**. These tell you the skills and knowledge you will be gaining in the chapter.
- **Skills and Capabilities Icons**. These show you at a glance where you have the opportunity to develop some cross-curricular skills. The icons are explained in the top table opposite.
- **Get Active**. These are tasks that help you improve your thinking and practise your skills in history.

- **Plan, Do, Review**. This helps you pull together all your work at the end of the chapter and gives you the opportunity to reflect on your own performance.
- **Key words**. These are highlighted in small capitals and defined in a glossary at the back of the book.

The last chapter in the book (Chapter 8) asks you to review your learning throughout the course. In order to do this you will need to draw on the knowledge, skills and experiences you have developed.

KEY ELEMENTS

Throughout your Key Stage 3 History course, you will also study aspects of the past that will help develop your understanding of the key elements of the curriculum, as shown in the bottom table opposite.

Skill/Capability	Icon	Description
Managing information		Research and manage information effectively to investigate historical issues, including identifying, collecting and using primary data/sources and accessing and interpreting a range of secondary sources.
Thinking, problem-solving, decision-making		Show deeper historical understanding, be more critical, think flexibly and make reasoned judgements.
Being creative		Demonstrate creativity and initiative when developing own ideas.
Working with others		Work effectively with others.
Self-management		Demonstrate self-management by working systematically, persisting with tasks, evaluating and improving own performance.

Key element	Description
Personal understanding	Explore how history has affected your personal identity, culture and lifestyle.
Mutual understanding	Investigate how history has been selectively interpreted to create stereotypical perceptions and to justify views and actions.
Personal health	Investigate how and why health standards have changed over time.
Moral character	Investigate individuals who are considered to have taken a significant moral stand and examine their motivation and legacy.
Spiritual awareness	Investigate and evaluate the spiritual beliefs and legacy of civilisations.
Citizenship	Investigate the long- and short-term causes and consequences of the partition of Ireland and how it has influenced Northern Ireland today, including key events and turning points.
Cultural understanding	Investigate the impact of significant events/ideas of the twentieth century on the world.
Media awareness	Critically investigate and evaluate the power of the media in their representation of a significant, historical event or individual.
Ethical awareness	Investigate ethical issues in history or historical figures who have behaved ethically or unethically.
Employability	Investigate how the skills developed through history will be useful in a range of careers, and the characteristics and achievements of entrepreneurs over time.
Economic awareness	Investigate the changing nature of local and global economies over time, and the impact of technology in the workplace over time.
Education for sustainable development	Investigate the need to preserve history in the local and global environment and evaluate the environmental impact of wars, industrial revolutions, etc.

Introduction: Welcome to the twentieth century!

There were many changes throughout the twentieth century that made the world at the end of it very different from at the beginning. This book is about some of these events, changes and turning points – some of which are shown on the timeline below.

GET ACTIVE 1

Think, pair, share

a Draw a table with three columns. At the top of the first column put **K**, at the top of the second column put **W** and in the last one put **L**.

b Can you think of two events or famous people from the twentieth century? Write them in the **K** column because this represents what you **K**now about the twentieth century.

c Listen to the feedback from your partner – what did they put in their **K** column? Add these to your table.

d Contribute and listen to the feedback from the rest of the class. What other events and/or people can you add to your **K** list?

e Now look at the second column in your table, the **W** column. What do you **W**ant to find out about the twentieth century? Add two questions you would like to have answered or two events you would like to find out more about. Share these with the rest of the class. Add on any other events to your second column that you had not thought of.

The **L** column is for what you have learned about the twentieth century. You can return to this at the beginning of Chapter 8 to fill in before you complete the course.

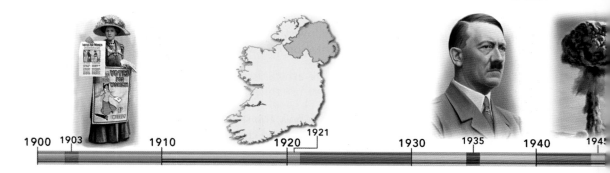

1900   1903   1910   1920   1921   1930   1935   1940   1945

1903	The Women's Social and Political Union – the 'Suffragettes' – was founded.
1921	Ireland was partitioned into two states.
1935	Adolf Hitler passed the Nuremburg Laws in Germany.
1945	The atomic bomb was dropped on Hiroshima.
1968	The My Lai massacre took place during the Vietnam War (1960–1973).
1969	The formation of the Provisional IRA.
1989	The fall of the Berlin Wall.

GET ACTIVE 2

Each of the events on the timeline below represents a key event or change covered in this book.

a Look at each event and match it with one of the following statements.

  i This event began the division of Ireland into a six-county northern state of Ulster and a 26-county southern state later known as the Republic.

  ii This caused millions to live in terror, and fear that a Third World War would be a nuclear holocaust. Ironically, however, it meant that the USA and the USSR kept the peace for the next half-century.

  iii Live coverage of events like this on television turned the American people against US involvement in the Vietnam War and led to many anti-war campaigns.

  iv In 1918 the Representation of the People Act gave voting rights to women of property over 30 years old.

  v This symbolised the end of the COLD WAR, the collapse of COMMUNISM as a world power, and the end of the nuclear-armed stand-off between the USA and the USSR.

  vi These acts were part of a series of official NAZI government policies that led to a systematic extermination of six million Jewish people.

  vii This event marked the beginning of 50 years of 'THE TROUBLES' in Northern Ireland.

b The words below are ones that historians use when describing why an event is *significant*. Choose from the list the most appropriate words or phrases that best describe the seven events on the timeline. Explain your choices to a partner and then decide whether you agree or disagree with the opening statement that the twentieth century was one of great change.

> led to … | first time | revolution | began
>
> widescale | pioneered | turned

You may find some of these words about significance useful in Chapters 1 and 4 when you are investigating why some events are more significant than others.

| 50 | 1960 | 1968 | 1969 / 1970 | 1980 | 1989 | 1990 | 2000 |

1 The twentieth century – an age of what?

In this chapter we are learning to:
- ✓ identify some of the key changes that took place during the twentieth century;
- ✓ understand that changes can be positive or negative;
- ✓ sort and classify information using historical terminology;
- ✓ work with others to produce a final outcome of a concept map, classifying some of the key changes of the twentieth century.

SOURCE 1

American astronaut Buzz Aldrin walks on the surface of the moon, 20 July 1969.

A CHANGING WORLD

The twentieth century saw remarkable changes in the way people in Ireland, Europe and other parts of the world lived their lives. From the start to the end of the century almost every aspect of life underwent change. In this chapter you will look at some of these changes and find out what people thought of them, in order to reach a conclusion about the question: 'The twentieth century – an age of what?'

The sources on pages 8–9 show some of the changes that happened during the twentieth century.

SOURCE 2

A modern Tomahawk cruise missile, armed with a 1,000 pound warhead, hits a warehouse-sized steel building with heavy concrete roof panels. The missile was launched from a submarine and has flown more than 400 miles to find its target.

SOURCE 3

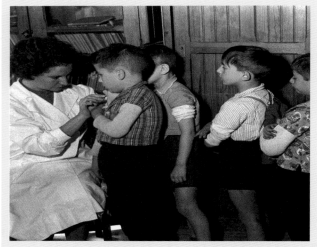

Children in Spain line up to be vaccinated against smallpox, 1961. In 1980, the UNITED NATIONS' World Health Organisation was able to declare the smallpox bacteria officially extinct.

GET ACTIVE 1

Sources 2 to 7 can be paired together to give examples of some of the changes that happened during the century. These changes can be put into categories; for example, one category might be 'warfare'.

a Match Sources 2 to 7 into appropriate pairs.
b Which source from each pair of sources is from the beginning of the century and which is from the end of the century?

c For each pair, suggest a category.
d What changes can you identify about the twentieth century from the three sets of sources?
e If you had to find your own source to match up with Source 1, what type of source would you look for? What category would you give the pair of sources? Can you come up with more than one answer?

SOURCE 4

The instrument of punishment at our school was the 'Strap', a length of leather, handle-shaped at one end, and cut into strip lashes at the other. But this was not for Mr Pell. He had his own special weapon, a short, thick stick about a foot long. The child was held firmly by the wrist while Pelly, bottom lip locked under the top teeth, whacked the stick down onto the palm of the outstretched hand. The rest of the class used to enjoy watching his spectacles jump about an inch off his nose as each stroke came down.

This description of punishment in school comes from the autobiography of Sid Manville, describing his childhood in Brighton between the wars.

SOURCE 5

Article 19: Governments should ensure that children are properly cared for, and protect them from violence, abuse and neglect by their parents or anyone else who looks after them.
Article 28: You have a right to an education. Discipline in schools should respect children's human dignity. Primary education should be free. Wealthy countries should help poorer countries achieve this.

An extract from the United Nations' Convention on the Rights of the Child (UNCRC), made in 1989 between United Nations member states (apart from the US and Somalia) about the human rights children should have.

SOURCE 6

Battle of the Somme, the Attack of the Ulster Division by J.P. Beadle is an image from the First World War. It shows the 36th Ulster Division climbing out of their trenches at the Battle of the Somme in 1916.

SOURCE 7

Chicago, April 22 – According to the latest 'Public Health Reports' of the United States' Marine Hospital Service, there were 7,648 cases and 402 deaths from smallpox in this country during the first three and a half months of the present year . . .

'And', says the Weekly Bulletin of the City Health Department, 'the end is not yet, every case of smallpox in Chicago during the past fifteen months . . . has, without exception, been unvaccinated. There has, thus far, been no case among the vaccinated.'

This article is from the New York Times, 24 April 1900.

GET ACTIVE 2

a List all the differences in lifestyle in 1900 and 2000 you can infer by studying Sources 1 and 2.

b Using the definitions in the box, categorise the changes on page 11 as 'political', 'social', 'economic' or 'cultural'.

c Do any of the changes fit more than one category?

d Carry out an internet image search – for example: 'in 1900 fashion' – to research images showing key changes in the twentieth century in areas which interest you (i.e., replace the word 'fashion' with topics that interest you, such as technology, music, entertainment, etc.).

e Try and identify which historical events influenced the changes you find.

CHANGING LIVES

On pages 8–9 you identified four changes that took place in Ireland, Europe or other parts of the world between 1900 and 2000. The table on page 11 outlines a dozen more major changes that happened in the United Kingdom over the period of the twentieth century.

Historians sometimes use specialist language to classify information. In particular, they often refer to historical events and changes as 'political', 'social', 'economic' or 'cultural'. The description of these terms is given in the box below.

 'Political' – the way in which the country is ruled/governed.

 'Social' – the type of lifestyle people have, and the relationships between people in a particular community. It can also include, for example, the types of homes people live in.

 'Economic' – the way in which people in a country earn their money, the sorts of jobs they do and their standard of living.

 'Cultural' – the way of life of a group of people, including the art and literature, pastimes and beliefs of a community. These are passed down from one generation to the next. Therefore, cultural identity can include traditions of dress, language and religion.

A family gathers for Christmas tea, c. 1900.

A modern family in their living room.

	At the beginning of the twentieth century . . .	By the end of the twentieth century . . .
Government	. . . the BRITISH EMPIRE covered one-fifth of the world, including India, many African countries, Canada, Australia and New Zealand.	. . . the British Empire had ceased to exist – former COLONIES had become independent. Many people from the former colonies emigrated to Britain.
	. . . all of Ireland was ruled directly from Britain.	. . . Ireland was PARTITIONED. The north was ruled as part of the United Kingdom, and the south had become the Republic of Ireland and was completely independent.
	. . . women and many men could not vote.	. . . Britain was a democracy in which all citizens over 18 could vote.
Travel	. . . people tended to live all of their lives in one country – many rarely left the village they had been born in.	. . . the mass production of the car had greatly increased the mobility of people. People lived in the suburbs and commuted to work in the city.
	. . . most people did not travel abroad unless they were very wealthy.	. . . many ordinary people travelled by airplane from one country to another.
Communication	. . . communication was largely by letter; some telegrams were sent but most people wrote to one another.	. . . email and the internet had changed the way that people communicated.
	. . . newspapers told people the news, sometimes days after it happened.	. . . developments in radio and television meant that people could see and hear about events as they were happening on the other side of the world.
Work	. . . many people made their living by working in heavy industries, such as the Harland and Wolff shipbuilding firm in Belfast.	. . . many more people worked in the service industry, for example in hotels such as the Merchant Hotel or the Europa Hotel in Belfast.
Housing	. . . many workers and their families lived in poor-quality, overcrowded accommodation near the factory they worked in.	. . . social housing – such as council houses – was provided from the 1940s and 50s onwards. There was an increase in the number of people buying their own homes.
Entertainment	. . . people in Britain went to the music halls for their entertainment. They could also go to watch silent movies in the cinema.	. . . most people watched the television at home. If they wanted to watch a movie, they could watch videos or DVDs at home.
Social issues	. . . the poor and unemployed had to go to the WORKHOUSE.	. . . the WELFARE STATE provided social security from the cradle to the grave.
	. . . issues such as concern for the environment or famine relief were up to individual charity.	. . . governments and international agencies raised awareness of social issues and took action.

DIFFERENT PERCEPTIONS

You have looked at some of the changes that took place in the twentieth century and have used categories to define the types of changes there were. Now you are going to look at what some different people have said about key aspects of the twentieth century.

Towards the end of the Second World War, the American government had developed the capability to produce nuclear weapons. Atomic bombs were dropped on the Japanese cities of Hiroshima and Nagasaki. The American government argued that this would, in effect, save American soldiers' lives as these events forced the Japanese to surrender.
The photograph shows an American reporter gazing at the wreckage of Hiroshima in 1945, after the atomic bomb had been dropped there.

GET ACTIVE 3

a How does the writer of Source 1 feel about the event he witnessed?

b What aspect of the twentieth century does Source 2 describe?

c List any differences you can find between Source 1 and Source 2. What different feelings about the twentieth century might the writer of Source 1 have to the writer of Source 2? Explain why they would have different feelings.

SOURCE 1

It was a horrible sight. Hundreds of injured people who were trying to escape passed our house. The sight of them was almost unbearable. Their faces and hands were swollen and great sheets of skin had peeled away from their tissues to hang down like rags on a scarecrow. This morning they had stopped. I found them lying on both sides of the road so thick it was impossible to pass without stepping on them.

Dr Tabuchi, a Japanese doctor, wrote this in his diary on 7 August 1945. He was describing what had happened after the Americans dropped the atomic bomb on Hiroshima.

SOURCE 2

For many people the twentieth century was a century of horror. It began with the Boer War, continued with the world wars and their atrocities and concluded with the ethnic cleansing in the Balkans. However, others look back at the century and remember great achievements like the moon landings and the technological advances that made such a difference to their everyday lives – such as the television and the washing machine. The twentieth century also saw great cultural changes with the 'Jazz Age', 'Rock and Roll' and the Punk movement.

A modern history teacher comments about the century as a whole.

GET ACTIVE 4

a In your exercise book draw a table with two columns for the 'Pros' (good things) and 'Cons' (bad things) of life in the twentieth century. Consider Sources 1 to 3, and use the information to put entries in both columns. Then, add further information from pages 10–13.
b From what you have learned so far, what is your initial impression of the twentieth century?

GET ACTIVE 5

a Draw a rollercoaster similar to the one shown on pages 16–17.
b Consider the list of facts on pages 16–17. Decide where to place each fact on the cars on your rollercoaster (the first has been done for you). Was it a good development that brought a positive change to people's lives, which you could place at a high point on the rollercoaster? Or was it a negative development that should be placed at a low point? Or did it have both good and bad aspects, so that you think it might come halfway?
   Also, some of the developments were the beginning of change for the better, and therefore you may wish to place them as climbing up. Or you might put them going down the track if you think they led to something negative. (Use arrows to show what direction events were moving in.)
c Explain reasons for your choices to a partner. Discuss and agree any changes you will make to the positions on the rollercoaster. Repeat this exercise in groups of four.

SOURCE 3

A gradually wider range of jobs has opened up to more women ... more recently, those giving access to real power – in the law, in banking, the civil service, as Prime Minister – for a very few, but still in numbers never known before.

Historian Pat Thane said this in 1988 about the impact of the twentieth century on the changing role of women in society.

THE TWENTIETH-CENTURY ROLLERCOASTER

As you have seen, the events of the twentieth century were varied. In fact, the whole century can be seen as a rollercoaster ride of ups and downs at different speeds. Some changes were good, others were terrible; some happened really quickly, while others happened gradually over a period of time.

12. **Famine**: during the twentieth century an estimated 70 million people died from famines.

6. **HIV/AIDS**: first recognised as a disease in 1981. By the end of the century an estimated 40 million people worldwide were living with, and some 20 million had died of AIDS.

3. **The National Health Service**: this was set up in Britain in 1948 so that people would have free medical care.

15. **Housing**: after the Second World War, council estates were built in Britain and Northern Ireland to provide social housing and many slum areas were demolished.

1. **Two World Wars**: and the death and destruction they brought.

11. **Women**: the position and status of women in the western world improved but although women made up over half the workforce in the USA, only three per cent held top jobs in businesses.

9. **Space**: the twentieth century could be called 'The Space Age'; for the first time man was able to walk on the moon.

7. **Genocide**: during the Second World War six million Jews and others were murdered by the Nazi state. There were other genocides too, for example in 1994 in Rwanda.

GET ACTIVE 6

a Find examples of local, national and global events on your rollercoaster.

b Find one event for each of the following categories: **political – social – economic – cultural**.

1. Two world wars: and the death and destruction they brought.

16. **The Troubles**: three thousand people died as a result of the Troubles in Northern Ireland, 1969–1998.

2. **Medicine**: many advances were made, for example antibiotics were developed to fight infection.

13. **The standard of living**: had improved for the majority of people in the western world by the end of the century.

8. **Schools**: at the end of the twentieth century still nearly 40 million children worldwide did not attend school.

5. **Poverty**: at the end of the twentieth century 3.8 million children (one in three) were living in poverty in Britain and many millions more around the world.

4. **Communications**: advances have allowed people all over the world to communicate more easily and quickly.

14. **Education**: in 1944 the Butler Education Act introduced free, compulsory education in Britain.

10. **Atomic energy**: among the greatest discoveries of the twentieth century, it was used for making both electricity and weapons.

SIGNIFICANT EVENTS OF THE TWENTIETH CENTURY

GET ACTIVE 7

a Judge the events described in Sources 1 to 4 against the six criteria that make an event significant. Choose the event that has been most significant.

b Imagine you are producing a television news story and could hot-seat one person from any of the events shown here. What questions would you ask them?

c Look back at pages 10–17. Find three more events that satisfy the criteria of being 'significant'. Explain your choices to a friend.

The twentieth century was made up of many different events. As you have seen, some of them led to positive change and others had negative effects.

When historians decide what to include in a study – such as in this book – they must decide if the event is significant. A significant event is one which:

1 affected a lot of people deeply;
2 changed people's lives forever;
3 tells us a lot about what was happening to people at a particular time;
4 without it, things would have turned out differently;
5 is still remembered;
6 still holds a valuable message for us in our world today.

The sources and information on these pages include four significant events of the twentieth century that had a moral or 'ethical' basis. You will study more significant events in Chapter 4.

SOURCE 1

Salt March, 1930

In the 1930s, India was part of the British Empire. One of the British rules was that the Indians could not make salt – they had to buy it (so that the British could take a tax on it). Mahatma Gandhi – to protest against this – made a 241-mile walk to the sea, followed by thousands of supporters. When he got there, he simply made a handful of salt. Thousands of others also disobeyed the law ... and the law was abolished.

Gandhi pioneered the principle of 'non-violent protest' that Martin Luther King (see page 17) and the 1989 Revolutions (see page 56) later used to change the world.

SOURCE 2

Hiroshima, 1945

In 1945, the USA dropped the atomic bomb on Hiroshima and Nagasaki. You studied its human effects on page 12. Although the Americans claimed that the bomb saved lives by shortening the war, the decision was described at the time as 'barbarism', and it contributed to a period called 'the Cold War', when people lived in fear of nuclear weapons.

SOURCE 3

'I Have a Dream' speech, 1963

Brought to America as slaves, black people had been regarded in parts of the USA as subhuman, and had been deprived of political and human rights. In the 1950s and 60s, a Baptist preacher called Reverend Martin Luther King led the Civil Rights Movement that won the vote for black people in America. His most remembered speech was given on 28 August 1963 at the Lincoln Memorial Washington DC: 'I have a dream that one day this nation will rise up and live out the true meaning of its creed: "We hold these truths to be self-evident: that all men are created equal ..."'

SOURCE 4

Live Aid, 1985

In 1985, a terrible famine in Ethiopia led Bob Geldof to mount Live Aid, a global charity pop concert held simultaneously on 13 July 1985 in London, Philadelphia and New York. The event was watched by more than 400 million people in 60 different countries. This was the first event of its kind. It not only inspired further celebrity charity events such as Red Nose Day, but it also saw a greater public demand for action in the less economically developed countries, which in turn led to significant government action such as the cancellation of some Third World debt.

GET ACTIVE 8

a Find a person to interview who was alive at the time of one of these events. Record or video this interview as a vox-pop to add to your television news story. Try to find out the person's opinions and emotions about the events, rather than simply asking questions that will lead to 'yes' or 'no' responses.

b The three events in Sources 1, 3 and 4 are clear examples of ethical action – good acts, by good people, done for good motives. Can you think of any other 'ethical' actions by individuals/ communities/ governments?

c Research the response to the use of the atomic bomb.

Plan, Do, Review

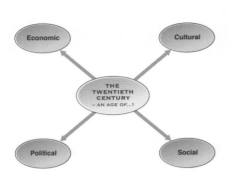

In this chapter you have been looking at the different types of events that took place during the twentieth century. You have seen that life for the majority of people was very different at the end of the century to what it had been before. You have also seen that the events and developments could be viewed differently and that some changes were for the better while others had a negative impact.

Now it is time to answer the question: 'The twentieth century – an age of what?' Your task is to produce a concept map – a collage of words and images – to answer this question.

After you have created your concept map you should use it to help you come to a conclusion about what the main events and changes of the twentieth century were. You should then be able to finish by completing the sentence: 'The twentieth century was an age of …'

PLAN

Stage 1

Get into groups of four and make a list of the tasks that need doing in order to produce your concept map and set time targets for each one. This will include gathering information, choosing what to include on your map, deciding how to present it to the rest of the class, etc.

Stage 2

As well as contributing to gathering the information and producing the concept map, each member of the group should take on one of the following roles:

Project manager – makes sure that everyone in the team has something to do and checks that they are doing it.

Timekeeper – ensures that group members keep to deadlines.

Quality controller – checks the quality of the work that is being done.

Presenter – will present your concept map to the rest of the class.

Stage 3

The concept map you create should categorise events and changes of the twentieth century you have studied into the following four headings:

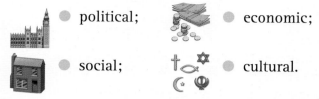

- political;
- economic;
- social;
- cultural.

Then divide your group so that one person is responsible for gathering information for each of the categories above.

Where events overlap into two or more categories, you will have to decide who is going to gather information on that event.

DO

As you prepare your presentation:

1 Give your team a name that relates to the twentieth century.
2 Produce your concept map using words and images from the century and historical terms such as 'political', 'social', 'economic' and 'cultural'.
3 Choose only the most significant events and developments.
4 Strengthen your final outcome by researching key events in more depth, using this chapter as a starting point for further research, and drawing conclusions based on the evidence you find.
5 Use images from the internet, your own drawings and newspaper and magazine clippings as well as text in your final concept map.
6 Use ICT to help in the research, production and presentation of your concept map.
7 Remember to make and explain the links between events/ developments that are connected on your concept map.
8 Present your findings about the twentieth century to the rest of your class, including an overall conclusion about the century and justification for your point of view.

REVIEW

Before the final presentation of your work, check that you have:

1 included some of the information from this chapter;
2 incorporated some of your own research using the internet and/or library and have listed your sources of information;
3 included both text and graphics in your concept map and have created a high-quality final outcome;
4 used historical terms accurately;
5 drawn a conclusion to the question and backed up your conclusion with reference to the sources from this chapter and your own knowledge.

② What impact did war have in the twentieth century?

In this chapter we are learning to:
✓ use a variety of sources to reach conclusions about warfare in the twentieth century;
✓ recognise and understand the impact of changes in twentieth-century warfare at a local and global level;
✓ work individually and with others to represent the key features of twentieth-century warfare.

SOURCE 1

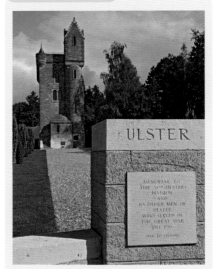

The Ulster Tower was built in 1921, in memory of those Ulstermen who died in the attack.

SOURCE 2

Part of a memorial window to the 36th Ulster Division, in Belfast City Hall.

THE 36th ULSTER DIVISION

The First World War 1914–1918 has been called the war to end all wars. It is remembered because of the terrible slaughter of young men in the trenches of Flanders. Soldiers from all over the world faced each other across the mud of 'NO MAN'S LAND'. The ULSTER DIVISION had been formed right at the beginning of the war and, like so many other divisions across the British Isles, it was made up of volunteers, brothers, cousins and friends from the same towns and villages.

The first day of the Battle of the Somme

At 7.30 a.m. on 1 July 1916, the 36th Ulster Division was among those which went 'over the top' in an attack on the German lines. The 13th Royal Irish Rifles formed the left flank of the Division's attack on the north bank of the river Ancre. The first wave of attackers had some success but later waves were cut to pieces by machine gun fire from the front and from the left across the valley. Pushed to their right and into the 11th Royal Irish Rifles, their attack was halted almost as soon as it had begun. However, on the other side of the river, the Ulster division, after ferocious fighting, successfully advanced to command the Schwaben Redoubt and five German trench lines. But the attack by the division on their right failed, and in consequence they found themselves under fire not only from the enemy in front of them, but also from German machine guns on their right. Their position could not be held. Fourteen hours later, the Germans had retaken the valley. More than 2,000 Ulstermen had died, 2,700 were wounded, and 165 had been taken prisoner. Of the nine VICTORIA CROSSES awarded on the first day of the Somme, three went to the Ulster Division (two POSTHUMOUSLY). The battle continued for another three months.

THE HUMAN FACTOR

The horror of the First World War is told in letters and poems written by soldiers at the front. These sources show how some soldiers reacted in the face of this terrible war.

A British soldier on lookout in the trenches in the First World War.

SOURCE 3

In February 1916, after an enemy grenade attack, Belfast volunteer James Crozier was found missing from his post, dazed and wandering about behind the line complaining of pains all over his body.

He was accused of desertion. His commanding officer reported that 'This soldier is of no value. His behaviour has been that of a "shirker" for the past three months.' On 27 February 1916 he was executed – 'in the interests of discipline'.

Later, his commanding officer wrote: 'He was no rotter deserving to die like that. He was merely fragile.'

SOURCE 4

I found a German, badly wounded. I could see from his face that he was mad with thirst. I gave him my water, although it was against orders. Then I found one of our men; he was terribly wounded … He begged me to kill him but I couldn't do it.

Lance-Corporal J.A. Henderson remembering what he did on the first day of the Battle of the Somme.

SOURCE 5

Dear Mother,
Just a few lines to let you know I am safe and thank God for it, for we had a rough time in the charge we made … Mother, we were tramping over the dead; I think there is only about 400 left out of about 1,300 … Mother, if God spares me to get home safely, I will have something awful to tell you. If hell is any worse I would not like to go to it. Mother, let me hear from you as soon as possible.
From your loving son Herbie.

A letter sent by Fusilier Herbert Beattie to his mother, soon after the attack at the Somme on 1 July 1916.

SOURCE 6

Gone like the snowflake that melts on the river
Gone like the first rays of day's early dawn
Like the foam from the fountain
Like the mist from the mountain
Young Billy McFadzean's dear life has gone

This song, still sung today, remembers Private William McFadzean, one of four Ulster soldiers who won the Victoria Cross at the Battle of the Somme. An apprentice at a Belfast linen company and a keen rugby player, he had written home: 'You people at home make me feel quite proud when you tell me "I am the Soldier Boy of the McFadzeans".' When – as the 36th Division prepared to attack on 1 July 1916 – two live grenades fell to the floor of the trench and exploded, William threw his body over them to save the rest of the men from being killed.

GET ACTIVE 1

Look at Sources 3 to 6.

a In what different ways did these young men react to the psychological stresses of battle? Are any of their reactions surprising?

b Look back at the six criteria for 'significance' on page 18. By these criteria, was the attack of the 36th Division on 1 July 1916 a 'significant' event?

c Use the internet to find out more about the Battle of the Somme and William McFadzean or James Crozier.

d Francis Ledwidge, from Slane, was one of the First World War poets. Use the internet to find out more about Francis and some of the poetry written by other soldiers at this time.

23

THE IMPACT OF TECHNOLOGY

Look at these pictures of tanks and planes from the First and Second World Wars.

SOURCE 1

A British Mark IV First World War tank. It was slow (top speed 4 mph) and clumsy, and frequently broke down. It had 1 millimetre plate steel armour, and four machine guns. Yet this clumsy machine helped bring an end to trench warfare.

SOURCE 2

A German Panzer tank from the Second World War. It had a top speed of 26 mph. It was protected by 80 millimetre steel plate armour, and had a machine gun and a 75 mm main gun which fired armour-piercing shells at 990 metres per second – making it effective at a range of almost two kilometres. It meant armies could advance into enemy territory faster than ever before.

SOURCE 3

This is a photo of the Fokker Triplane used by Manfred von Richthofen, the 'Red Baron' of Germany, who shot down 80 Allied airplanes during the First World War. The plane was slow (top speed 155 mph), and subject to engine and wing failures. It was fitted with two machine guns. The average life span of a young pilot in the First World War was just three weeks. The ability to photograph and bomb enemy positions from the air changed the way wars were fought.

SOURCE 4

Spitfires and Hurricanes were the planes that saved Britain during the Battle of Britain in the Second World War. The Spitfire had a top speed of 378 mph and was armed with eight machine guns and two 250 lb bombs.

Winston Churchill, the British Prime Minister, paid tribute to the pilots when he said in a famous speech in August 1940 that 'Never in the field of human conflict was so much owed by so many to so few.'

SOURCE 5

An RAF Lancaster bomber, the workhorse of Bomber Command during the Second World War. Lancasters flew 156,000 sorties and dropped 608,612 tons of bombs between 1942 and 1945. They had a top speed of 280 mph and a range of 3,000 miles. The bouncing bombs in the famous Dambusters raid were dropped from a Lancaster bomber.

Both sides in the war used bombers like the Lancaster to target civilian populations as well as military targets.

The Belfast Blitz

During the Second World War, far away from Germany, the people of Belfast did not expect Nazi air raids. There were only 200 air raid shelters, no anti-aircraft guns, and no children had been EVACUATED, as they had been from London.

On the night of 15–16 April 1941, 180 German bombers attacked for two hours, dropping 203 tons of bombs and 800 fire-bomb canisters; more than 900 people died. And in an even bigger raid on the night of 4–5 May 1941, 205 German bombers dropped 95,992 fire-bombs and 237 tons of high explosive – Belfast suffered more devastation in one night than in the 30 years of the Troubles after 1969. Perhaps half the city's houses were damaged, and a quarter of the population were made homeless.

Belfast city centre after the Belfast Blitz.

Emma Duffin, a Belfast nurse who had served in the First World War, was horrified at what she saw:

SOURCE 6

I had seen young men dying of ghastly wounds, but nothing I had ever seen was as terrible as this ... [First World War soldiers] had died in hospital beds, their eyes had been reverently closed, their hands crossed to their breasts. Death had to a certain extent been ... made decent, but here it was grotesque, repulsive, horrible ... With tangled hair, staring eyes, clutching hands, contorted limbs, their grey-green faces covered with dust, they lay ... still wearing their dirty, torn and twisted garments. Death should be dignified, peaceful; Hitler had made even death grotesque. I felt outraged, I should have felt sympathy, grief, but instead feelings of revulsion and disgust assailed me.

Emma Duffin wrote this in her diary.

GET ACTIVE 2

Look at Sources 1 to 5.

a Discuss with a partner about how technology changed the way that the First and Second World Wars were fought.
b Explain how the events of the Belfest Blitz were a direct result of one of the changes illustrated on page 24.
c Study Source 6. What were Emma Duffin's feelings about the changes in warfare?
   • How reliable do you think Source 6 is as a record of what happened that night?
   • How is it useful to historians studying the Belfast Blitz?
d Using the internet, find out more about the Belfast Blitz of 1941.

A list of countries involved in the First World War:

Albania
Arabia
Australia
Austria–Hungary
Belgium
Brazil
Bulgaria
Canada
China
Costa Rica
Cuba
Czechoslovakia
Estonia
Finland
France
Germany
Great Britain and Ireland
Greece
Guatemala
Haiti
Honduras
Italy
Japan
Latvia
Liberia
Lithuania
Luxembourg
Montenegro
New Zealand
Nicaragua
Panama
Persia
Philippines
Poland
Portugal
Romania
Russia
San Marino
Serbia
Siam
South Africa
Transcaucasia
Turkey
United States of America

GLOBAL IMPACT

The twentieth century was the first century to see war fought on a global scale with soldiers from all over the world involved in the same war at the same time. For example, in both World Wars soldiers from Belfast or Glasgow fought alongside soldiers from India or Australia. This meant that many countries and peoples shared the human cost of war.

SOURCE 2

Australian and New Zealand Corps (ANZAC) charge a Turkish trench at Gallipoli in Turkey in the First World War in 1915. In Australia and New Zealand, Anzac Day is commemorated on the 25 April every year to remember those who fought and died at Gallipoli.

SOURCE 3

The American war cemetery near Omaha Beach in Normandy, France. Every white dot is the grave of one of the thousands of American soldiers who died in the D-Day landings of the Second World War on 6 June 1944.

SOURCE 4

In any war you have combatants – those who fight – and civilians – those who are not directly involved in the conflict. The technology of twentieth-century warfare meant that civilian populations were more in danger than ever before. On the night of 9–10 March 1945, American bombers dropped a million fire-bombs on Tokyo, Japan. The fire consumed the air so that many people who were not burned to death suffocated to death.

In August 1945 the Americans dropped a new, more lethal bomb – the atomic bomb – on two Japanese cities. The destruction of Hiroshima and Nagasaki forced the Japanese to surrender on 12 August 1945.

SOURCE 5

War deaths represented one in eight of the six million men from the British Isles who had served in the Great War (1914–1918) ... This gave rise to the idea of a 'lost generation' ... According to one estimate, 30.58 per cent of all men aged twenty to twenty-four in 1914 were killed and 28.15 per cent of those aged thirteen to nineteen.

John Stevenson, Social History of Britain: British Society, 1914–45 *(1990)*.
When he wrote this, John Stevenson was Reader in History at the University of Sheffield.

SOURCE 6

So many men had died in the First World War that in villages, towns and cities all over the world, war memorials were erected listing the names of the men from that area who had lost their lives. This photo shows the war memorial at Dungannon, Co. Tyrone. It records the names of 200 men who died in the First World War.

GET ACTIVE 3

a What evidence do Sources 1 to 6 provide to support the view that the two World Wars were fought on a global scale involving countries from many parts of the world?

b Use the internet to find a list of the 'Participants in the Second World War'.

c Carry out a class or group enquiry to find evidence of the impact of the two World Wars on your own town or village.
  • Look for the physical evidence of the wars (for example, in plaques in churches, statues, etc.).
  • Photograph your local war memorial and count the number of men's names inscribed.
  • Use your evidence to prepare a presentation about some of the people who fought in the World Wars in your area.

REPORTING WAR

Twentieth-century technology increased the speed and the means by which news from war zones could be dispatched to and viewed by people back at home. The images of war became more instant and began to change the way people thought about what was happening.

SOURCE 1

During the First World War (1914–1918), leading newspapers took advantage of the rotogravure printing process, which allowed them to produce detailed, high-quality illustrations, even on cheap paper. This is a rotogravure image of French and British soldiers reading the rotogravure section of the New York Times, 23 May, 1915. People at home began to understand the horror of the trenches.

SOURCE 2

During the Second World War, Pathé News kept the home front informed about the war overseas. People went to their local cinema to watch moving images of the war.

However, the government could still keep strict control of what people saw and used the films to keep up morale and show the enemy in a bad light.

SOURCE 3

The Vietnam War was the first war to be watched on TV. The American public went home every night and watched shocking images of the war – such as this one of Vietnamese children burned in an accidental napalm attack on a 'friendly' village. As a result, many turned against the war.

SOURCE 4

The First Gulf War in 1991 was the first 'live' televised war, and 24-hour live coverage meant that viewers all round the world could watch events as they unfolded. Teachers and parents reported that children were being traumatised by a war that seemed to them very near.

SOURCE 5

A policeman gives a cup of tea to a dejected and tired-looking man whose house has just been destroyed by a Nazi V2 rocket (c.1944). In the background, rescue workers search the wreckage for survivors; the blast zone is huge and the destruction total. Behind him, a few blankets are all he has been able to salvage of his belongings.

The comment below, by John Swain who has reported on every major war since 1970, highlights the power of war-reporting to affect what people think about war.

SOURCE 6

Powerful writing and powerful pictures will not stop wars, but they are valuable because they make it more difficult for the world to close its eyes to human suffering.

Jon Swain, journalist, quoted in The Sunday Times, 6 July 2008.

GET ACTIVE 4

a Use Sources 1 to 4 to explain how war-reporting changed during the twentieth century.

b Read Source 6. Why does Jon Swain think his work as a news reporter is valuable? Talk about images of war that have had an impact on you.

c During wartime, governments have CENSORED information coming from the front line. Suggest reasons why, during war time, governments might not want the public back at home to view 'powerful writing and powerful pictures'.

d It is 1944. You are a war reporter who has to write an article on the scene in Source 5. You want to act responsibly, but you also want to write a powerful article to accompany the picture. Discuss with a partner what considerations you need to take into account, and how you should write the article.

NATIONS AGAINST WAR

On pages 28–33 you are going to study the various attempts made by nations, societies and individuals to prevent war or help those caught up in war.

1 UNITED NATIONS AGAINST WAR

Throughout history countries have joined together in alliances to make themselves stronger and more prepared to fight and defend themselves in a war. The twentieth century was the first century when nations, large and small, from across the world, came together to create an organisation to work for world peace.

The first attempt was in 1919, when 42 countries formed the LEAGUE OF NATIONS. And in the aftermath of the Second World War (a war in which more people had been killed than in any previous war in history), the nations of the world came together to create a much stronger organisation called the UNITED NATIONS.

Its founding charter declared:

SOURCE 1

We, the Peoples of the United Nations, determined to save succeeding generations from the scourge of war, which twice in our lifetime has brought untold sorrow to mankind … have resolved to combine our efforts to accomplish these aims.

Preamble to the Charter of the United Nations, signed in San Francisco, California on 26 June, 1945, by 50 nations of the United Nations.

The United Nations member states are represented by a parliament of nations called the General Assembly, which meets in New York. Each member state has one vote. A smaller group of 15 nations, called the Security Council, meets to discuss action to prevent or stop wars and reduce the dangers posed by powerful weapons. The United Kingdom is a permanent member of the Security Council.

The United Nations General Assembly

A UNICEF-assisted child reunification centre in Democratic Republic of Congo

Members of the UNDOF Polish contingent on patrol

How does the United Nations work for peace?

1 The World Health Organisation seeks to promote world health. It led the immunisation campaign, which wiped out smallpox, and now it is trying to work against AIDS.

2 The UN Disaster Relief Office (UNDRO) works with organisations such as the Red Cross to send aid when there are natural disasters.

3 In 2000, the UN agreed eight 'Millennium Goals' to be achieved by 2015, including ending extreme poverty, providing primary education for all children, promoting gender equality and stopping AIDS.

4 UN peacekeeping forces have been sent to areas of conflict or disaster to help protect civilian populations.

5 The Food and Agriculture Organisation tries to defeat world hunger.

6 The International Criminal Court was set up in 2002 to try people accused of war crimes.

7 UNESCO (the United Nations Educational, Scientific and Cultural Organisation) sponsors cultural and scientific projects. It also declares areas of great cultural importance 'world heritage sites' (such as the Giant's Causeway).

8 On 10 December 1948 the UN assembly passed the Universal Declaration of Human Rights which declared that: 'Everyone has the right to life, liberty and security of person.' The UN's Human Rights Council exposes and condemns human rights violations.

9 The UN has agreed a number of significant disarmament agreements, e.g. treaties prohibiting the development of chemical and bacteriological weapons. Also, in 1997 the Ottawa Convention outlawed the use of landmines.

10 The Permanent Court of International Justice makes decisions on disagreements between nations, such as over borders, or land.

11 UNICEF, the United Nations Children's Fund, works for children's rights, and their survival, development and protection.

12 The UN has worked to reduce the danger to mankind posed by nuclear weapons, e.g. the Nuclear-Test-Ban-Treaty in 1996.

GET ACTIVE 5

a All the UN agencies described on this page contribute to keeping the peace. Working with a partner, discuss how each agency plays its part in promoting a peaceful world.

b Still working with your partner, use the information on this page to build a concept map showing how the United Nations works to keep the peace. Remember to show the links between the agencies, as well as the links to peace.

c Using the internet, find out more about one of the agencies. Prepare a poster encouraging pupils at your school to value its work.

13 The International Atomic Energy Agency seeks to promote the use of nuclear energy for peaceful purposes.

14 The UN's Economic and Social Council (ECOSOC) promotes international cooperation.

2 ORGANISATIONS WHO SUPPORT VICTIMS OF WAR

During the twentieth century many independent organisations have been formed to raise awareness of humanitarian issues and help those affected by war and disasters.

SOURCE 1

The Red Cross

 International Federation of Red Cross and Red Crescent Societies

Founded in 1919, the International Federation comprises 186 member Red Cross and Red Crescent societies, a Secretariat in Geneva and more than 60 delegations strategically located to support activities around the world with the help of millions of volunteers. There are more societies in formation. The Red Crescent is used in place of the Red Cross in many Islamic countries. The International Federation of Red Cross and Red Crescent Societies is the world's largest humanitarian organisation, providing assistance without discrimination as to nationality, race, religious beliefs, class or political opinions.

A violent civil war reached the country of Rwanda in 1994. Refugees fled from the dangers of militias, and were helped by the International Committee of the Red Cross which coordinates the response of national Red Cross societies in situations of conflict.

SOURCE 2

Amnesty International

We are a movement of ordinary people from across the world standing up for humanity and human rights. Our purpose is to protect individuals wherever justice, fairness, freedom and truth are denied. With more than 2.5 million members, we can produce extraordinary results – prisoners of conscience released, death sentences commuted, torturers brought to justice, governments persuaded to change unfair laws and practices.

This quote and logo are taken from the Amnesty International website.

Amnesty International campaigns for political prisoners and victims of faith. Here, supporters demonstrate in London about the detention without trial of suspected terrorists in Guantánamo Bay prison by the USA.

SOURCE 3

Campaign for Nuclear Disarmament

There had been 'Ban the Bomb' marches in Britain since the 1950s, but in 1981 a large group of women gathered at Greenham Common, Berkshire, to challenge the placing of 96 US Cruise nuclear missiles there.

When they were ignored they stayed – for 19 years.

In the end, they won; the Cruise missiles were taken back to the USA in 1987, and in 2000 the military base was closed down.

SOURCE 4

Nobel Peace Prize

Throughout history many people have tried to be peacemakers but it was not until the twentieth century that such efforts were celebrated and acknowledged in a formal way. Having made a fortune from the invention of dynamite, the Swedish industrialist Alfred Nobel left a huge sum of money in his will to fund an annual prize to be given to a person who has done most for the promotion of peace.

The first Nobel Peace Prize was awarded in 1901 and was shared by Frédéric Passy (the founder of an international Interparliamentary Union) and Jean Henri Dunant (founder of the Red Cross in Switzerland).

Other famous winners have included Martin Luther King (1964), Mother Teresa (1979), Mikhail Gorbachev (1990) and Nelson Mandela (1993).

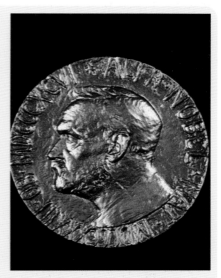

Medal given to the Nobel Peace Prize winner.

GET ACTIVE 6

a Organisations such as the Red Cross or Amnesty International are often described as non-government organisations or NGOs. Suggest why it is important that such groups are neutral and free to speak out in a society.

b Look at the Amnesty logo opposite. What do you think the candle and barbed wire represent? What logo would you choose to represent an organisation supporting people in conflict? Discuss and agree on a suitable logo.

c Carry out research on the internet.
   i Find out why Martin Luther King, Mother Teresa, Mikhail Gorbachev and Nelson Mandela were awarded the Nobel Peace Prize.
   ii Find out more about the histories of the Red Cross, Amnesty International and the Campaign for Nuclear Disarmament. Use your research to create a poster about one of these organisations.

SOURCE 1

The only Victoria Cross won by an Ulsterman during the Second World War is soon to make a rare public appearance. The VC [was] awarded to sailor James Magennis from Belfast for his bravery ... in a dangerous underwater action in July 1945. The daring of Magennis that July night has been compared to fictional tales of daring by James Bond, and author Ian Fleming is said to have had Magennis in mind when he was writing his early novels.

There is a memorial to Magennis in the grounds of Belfast City Hall which was unveiled in 1999.

From the Belfast Telegraph, *15 July 2008. Magennis was awarded the Victoria Cross for great bravery in attaching limpet mines to a Japanese warship.*

3 INDIVIDUALS WHO TOOK A STAND

The twentieth century provides many examples of times when individuals have acted with courage and performed acts of heroism during wartime. Sometimes they are given medals or even have plaques or memorials erected to them. Sometimes, however, courage is shown through acts of resistance or defiance against the cruelty of war.

Harry Stanton, conscientious objector

A CONSCIENTIOUS OBJECTOR is a person who refuses to fight in a war. In the First World War, especially, they were treated very harshly by most people, who regarded them as traitors and cowards.

Harry Stanton, from Luton, was a PACIFIST (he did not believe in violence), so when he was called up into the army in 1916, he refused to go. He was taken to France anyway. Once there, he was made to line up with the soldiers. But when military drill began, he refused to move.

He was punished for disobeying military orders. First, he was moved to a field punishment camp for 28 days, where he was tied by the arms to a cross. Next, he was imprisoned and handcuffed with 16 other men in a timber cage roughly 12 feet square. Finally, in June, he was taken to Henriville military camp for COURT MARTIAL, and sentenced to death.

Henry was not executed. His sentence was commuted to ten years' penal servitude. He was sent to do manual labour at a work camp near Aberdeen. Harry decided that by working, he was freeing up other men to join the army. So he refused to work at all, and was sent to prison until the war ended in 1919.

GET ACTIVE 7

a Make list of how each of the individuals featured on pages 34–5, reacted to war and the consequences they faced.
b 'If everybody agrees that war is so terrible – why don't they just stop?' Discuss this idea in class. Why DO countries still fight wars when the human cost is so great?
c Harry Stanton and Hugh Thompson would have faced criticism for their actions. Organise a class hot-seat – half prepare questions and half prepare possible responses for Harry and Hugh.

Hugh Thompson, the pilot who broke ranks

In the Vietnam War, one American soldier took a brave stand against his own side to protect innocent villagers who were being massacred by American soldiers.

In March 1968, a platoon of American soldiers led by Lieutenant William Calley ran amok in a small Vietnamese village called My Lai, massacring the old men, women and children they had found there.

The massacre was witnessed by an army helicopter pilot named Hugh Thompson. He landed, placed himself in between the soldiers and the villagers, and ordered his men to shoot any soldier who killed a civilian. He rescued as many Vietnamese as he could, getting them flown out to hospital. And then – despite being called a traitor by many Americans – he bravely testified at Calley's trial to what had happened.

'There was no thinking about it,' he said later. 'There was something that had to be done, and it had to be done fast.'

Hugh Thompson, attending to give evidence at the trial of William Calley in 1970. For a time, he feared that it was he, instead, who was going to be courtmartialled.

Diana, the People's Princess

Landmines used to be planted by the thousands during twentieth-century wars. Hidden under the soil, they exploded under the feet of any soldier unlucky enough to stand on one. They were not designed to kill, but rather they were designed to injure and maim – the object was to tie up enemy medical staff in long operations. Often, they were made of plastic, so that the shards would not show up under X-ray.

In January 1997, five months after she divorced Prince Charles, Princess Diana made a trip to Angola in Africa to see the effects of landmines, and to speak out against them.

She was criticised by the government, who called her 'ill-informed' and 'a loose cannon'.

But an international petition to ban landmines in 1997 collected 855,000 signatures and, one month after Diana's death, the British Prime Minister at the time, Tony Blair, promised to ratify a United Nations treaty banning landmines.

> **SOURCE 2**
>
> Ten years after the death of Princess Diana and the first Global Treaty against anti-personnel landmines, experts say only a handful of rebel groups and perhaps one state dare use what has become a pariah weapon.
>
> *Reuters International News Agency, London, 16 July 2007.*

Princess Diana meets a young landmine victim on her visit to Angola.

Plan, Do, Review

WHAT IMPACT DID WAR HAVE IN THE TWENTIETH CENTURY?

This chapter has studied certain aspects of twentieth-century warfare. You have looked at the impact of wars on the people who fought in them, and on the people who stayed at home. You have considered the impact of new technology on how and where wars were fought. You have studied how wars have been reported, and at the work of governments, society and individuals to prevent wars and help those caught up in them.

Your task now is to use the information and skills you have learned to create a piece of work – a collage of information about the impact of war in the twentieth century.

This could be an individual or group task and will require a lot of planning and research. You have complete freedom to decide what shape your final presentation will take. You could choose to create a poster, with images and headlines from across the century; you might decide to create a short film or photo story with images about a specific event. Alternatively, a song or poem would also be an excellent way of expressing your feelings and illustrating your understanding of some of the key features of the impact of war in the twentieth century.

PLAN

Stage 1 – choose your topic
- Look back through the chapter to decide what you will focus on, for example:
  - Has a specific event or personal story captured your imagination?
  - Have you noticed a development or change that seems very important?
- Agree the success criteria for your work and how you will evaluate the finished piece, for example:
  - It must focus on the impact of war.
  - It must show both local and global examples.
  - It must include examples of individual as well as national action.

Stage 2 – collect your evidence
Begin by examining the evidence throughout this chapter.
- Working in pairs, copy the table opposite. Now work back through the chapter and list the sources, images and other information you could use in your piece of work. Add these to your table. Be selective and justify your choices.

- After you have listed your evidence in your table decide whether it is primary (first-hand accounts and documents such as eye-witness statements) or secondary evidence (information produced by historians after the event), and how reliable it is. This will help you to organise your evidence as you come to prepare your presentation.
- You may decide to do extra research on the internet or in your local library.

Sources we have chosen	Reasons for choice – usefulness/evidence it provides/what it shows	Category – primary or secondary	Reliability

Stage 3 – plan your work

- Now you must organise the materials you have collected so that they will have maximum impact in your presentation. This might be:
  - organised into chronological order;
  - analysed into categories of evidence/impact;
  - arranged for maximum visual or emotional impact.

DO

- Having collected and organised all your evidence, and thought about your success criteria, now produce your final piece of work. Think carefully about:
  - the information you want to communicate;
  - the feelings you want to evoke.
- Remember that the presentation is about the physical and psychological IMPACT of war, so – whatever your subject – make sure you finish with a conclusion that sums up WHAT the impact was, on WHOM, WHERE, and WHY it was significant.
- Be prepared to present your work and talk about what it means. If you have been working in groups, then each of you will need to agree and plan your individual roles in the presentation.

REVIEW

Compare and contrast your presentation with the others produced by your class.

- Which events/developments did you choose as the most significant and why? Make a note of how the others made their choices.
- What pleased you about your presentation? What really worked well? What would you change and how could you improve your work?

3 How should we remember the Holocaust?

In this chapter we are learning to:
- ✓ understand why the Holocaust happened;
- ✓ select, use and combine sources and own information to draw conclusions about the significance of the Holocaust;
- ✓ make reasoned judgements based on sound evidence.

HOLOCAUST MEMORIAL DAY

The logo from the 2009 Holocaust Memorial Day event.

We recognise that the Holocaust shook the foundations of modern civilisation . . .

We believe the Holocaust must have a permanent place in our nation's collective memory. We honour the survivors still with us . . .

We must make sure that future generations understand the causes of the Holocaust and reflect upon its consequences.

We vow to remember the victims of Nazi persecution and of all genocide.

From the HMD Statement of Commitment, 2009.

The Holocaust describes the FINAL SOLUTION, which was the last step in a series of anti-Jewish actions carried out by the Nazi regime in Germany between 1933 and 1945. It was the planned extermination of the Jews from 1941 onwards which resulted in the GENOCIDE of over six million Jewish people. As well as targeting Jews, the Nazis tried to eliminate other groups of people they considered to be undesirables, such as gypsies, homosexuals and people with disabilities. Many Jewish people use the word Shoah instead of Holocaust. This means a whirlwind and is an Old Testament term for widespread destruction.

Holocaust Memorial Day (HMD) is an annual day of remembrance, when people and organisations from all over the world hold events to remember the victims of the Holocaust, to honour the survivors, and to promise to oppose the prejudice, discrimination and racism that exists in the world today. As well as remembering victims of the Holocaust and Nazi persecution, HMD also commemorates subsequent genocides in Cambodia, Bosnia, Rwanda and Darfur. The events are held on 27 January, because that is the date when the Auschwitz–Birkenau death camp was liberated by Russian soldiers at the end of the Second World War.

SOURCE 1

Soon after liberation, an emaciated child survivor is carried out of camp barracks by Soviet first-aid workers. Auschwitz, Poland, after 27 January, 1945.

SOURCE 2

Wal and I decided to tell younger generations our stories to warn them about the human capacity for inhuman behaviour. This behaviour is not carried out by invading monsters but more often than not by ordinary people. Both of us feel it is important to speak to as many people as we can about PREJUDICE and DISCRIMINATION and hope they can learn from our experiences.

Holocaust survivor Ibi Ginsberg explains why she and her husband tell their story to school pupils.

SOURCE 3

A photo from the Auschwitz–Birkenau Museum showing visitors looking at photographs of families and people who were killed there.

SOURCE 4

When the Nazis came for the Communists,
I remained silent;
I was not a Communist.
Then they locked up the Socialists,
I remained silent;
I was not a Socialist.
Then they came for the trade unionists,
I did not speak out;
I was not a trade unionist.
Then they came for the Jews,
I did not speak out;
I was not a Jew.
When they came for me,
there was no one left to speak out for me.

A poem about the Holocaust written by a German pastor, Martin Niemoller, and published in a book in 1955.

GET ACTIVE 1

Study the sources on this page.
a What do all the sources tell us about the victims of the Holocaust?
b Look again at Source 2. Why does the survivor feel it is important to tell the story of the Holocaust?
c With a partner now think of any questions you would like to ask about the Holocaust. Use the five Ws to help you organise your questions (Who? What? Where? Why? When?).

HOW WERE JEWISH PEOPLE TREATED IN GERMANY BEFORE 1933?

Jewish people counted for less than one per cent of the German population – in 1933, there were about 500,000 Jews in a population of 67 million. Eighty per cent of them (400,000) were full German citizens. Many were wealthy and middle class.

For centuries, Europe's Jews had been attacked and persecuted on both religious and racial grounds. This is called ANTI-SEMITISM. At the end of the nineteenth century, there had been 'POGROMS' in Russia attacking Jewish property and driving out Jews from their homes.

However, in Germany in the 1890s there was an anti-Semitic movement, which tried to get Jews excluded from politics; it failed. After 1900, Jewish people became more and more part of German society and began to mix with ordinary Germans, both socially and politically. Many of them had become local mayors and councillors and one of Germany's leading politicians in the 1920s, Gustav Stresemann, had a Jewish wife.

SOURCE 1

Martin Farntrog poses in the garden with his three daughters and two of their friends. Martin had settled in Germany and lived in Nuremberg. During the First World War he had fought for the German Army and won the Iron Cross, the highest military honour.

SOURCE 2

Of half a million Jews in Germany, 100,000 fought for their country in the First World War, 12,000 died and 30,000 were awarded medals. When, after the war, the legend grew up that the Jews had caused Germany's defeat, the Reich Association of Jewish Front Soldiers published this poster which says: '12,000 Jewish soldiers died for their country on the field of honour'.

SOURCE 3

Of Germany's Jews in the years before 1933:
- 62 per cent worked in business or commerce;
- 46 per cent were self employed or worked in the family business;
- 1 in 10 doctors and 1 in 7 lawyers were of Jewish descent;
- The majority of Berlin banks and department stores were Jewish-owned;
- Jewish companies dominated the clothing, tobacco, leather and fur industries;
- The editors of Germany's two biggest newspapers were Jewish;
- Jewish people were prominent in the theatre and film industry;
- Jewish factory owners employed many non-Jewish workers.

GET ACTIVE 2

a Study Sources 1–3 and make a list of all the ways in which Jewish people contributed successfully to German society.

b How would these successes have helped Jewish people feel they belonged in Germany?

c Look carefully at Source 3. Why might non-Jewish Germans feel resentful of the Jews?

THE RISE OF THE NAZI PARTY

In the last section you may have realised that while many Jewish people were integrated into different levels of German society, there were still some Germans who had anti-Semitic views. However, it was the rise of a small political party in the 1920s, later called the Nazis, led by Adolf Hitler, that was to have great influence on Germany's attitudes towards the Jews. Hitler began to openly criticise and blame the Jews for causing Germany's problems at that time. Pages 40–1 explain who Hitler was and why people came to support his ideas.

Adolf Hitler was born in Austria in 1889. When he was 18 he went to Vienna to become an artist. He was very poor, and this may be where his hatred of Jewish money-lenders began.	In the First World War (1914–1918) Hitler fought for the German Army, where he won the Iron Cross twice. He blamed the Jews for the surrender and defeat of Germany.	In 1923 Hitler tried to seize power but was thrown in prison instead. There he wrote these words in his book *Mein Kampf*: 'The Germans are the Master Race. No Jews may be members of the nation.'	After 1924, Hitler tried to gain power by democratic means. He gave speeches attacking the Communists and the Jews. But the Nazi party did not do well in the elections.

In 1929 the **WALL STREET CRASH** in America led to the **GREAT DEPRESSION** and the collapse of many German businesses. Unemployment soared. Hitler promised the German people that the Nazis would end unemployment and make Germany great again. Many Germans voted for him, and in 1932 the Nazis became the biggest party in the German Parliament, the Reichstag.

In 1933 President Hindenburg invited Hitler to become Chancellor of Germany. Hitler used his power to give himself the right to make laws, ban all opposition parties, take over the police, and arrest and kill his opponents. When Hindenburg died in August 1934, Hitler declared himself **FÜHRER** or leader of Germany.

WHY DID SO MANY GERMANS SUPPORT THE NAZI PARTY?

Can you remember 1923? Prices went up and up – my pension was worthless and I was ruined. Hitler says he will improve pensions.

A pensioner

We have all lost our jobs because of the Great Depression. Hitler says he will give us jobs. I would vote for the Devil if he gave me a job.

A factory worker

There is chaos and violence everywhere – Communists fighting Nazis. Hitler has promised us law and order.

A middle-class housewife

Hitler was a soldier and a hero. Hitler is right – the Jews betrayed us in the Great War! Now the other countries are making us pay millions for our defeat. Hitler says he will make Germany powerful again.

An ex-soldier

This government is weak – there are too many elections and different parties. We need a strong leader to knock this country into shape.

A judge

Hitler has promised to win back the territory stolen from us after the Great War. He will make Germany great again.

A stormtrooper

Have you seen the nightclubs, the homosexuals, and those 'new women' who smoke cigarettes? Degenerates! Hitler says he will bring back good old German values.

An elderly Protestant minister

With all this unemployment I'm worried the Communists will take over, and I'll lose my business. Hitler wants to destroy the Communists.

A rich businessman

I don't like the Nazis, but if you don't give them money, these stormtroopers, they come round and threaten you. So it's safer to support them.

A small businessman

GET ACTIVE 3

a Use the talking heads above to explain why people voted for Hitler and the Nazi Party.

b Reading Hitler's story on page 42:

  i   List the things Hitler did to get power.

  ii Is there anything in Hitler's early career to show that he did not like the Jews?

  iii Initially, the Nazi party was not successful in the elections. Why might the Great Depression have made people more likely to vote for Hitler?

HOW WERE THE JEWS TREATED IN NAZI GERMANY?

Look at these photographs, all of which might have come from a Jewish person's scrapbook of the time. They give information about what was happening to Jews in Germany and the countries occupied by the Nazis during the Second World War. They are not in chronological order.

1933: the Nazis urged Germans to boycott Jewish businesses. Here, Germans gather in front of a Jewish-owned department store in Berlin on the first day of the boycott. Stormtroopers deter shoppers. The poster reads: 'Germans! Defend yourselves! Don't buy from Jews!'

On the night of 9 November 1938, Nazi mobs burned the synagogues, beat up Jews and broke windows (which was why the night was called *Kristallnacht* – 'glass night'). Twenty thousand Jews were deported and 91 were killed. This picture shows a Jewish department store the next day.

After 1941, all Jews were forced to wear a yellow Star of David, to identify them as a Jew.

1935: this German woman (who had dated a Jew) is displayed in public wearing a sign that says: 'I am the greatest swine in the world and only get involved with Jews'.

1942: here thousands of German Jews are being deported to extermination camps, such as Auschwitz in Poland.

1938: these two Jewish children have been brought to the front of the class so the teacher can point out their 'subhuman' physical features. The text on the blackboard reads: 'The Jews are our greatest enemy'.

7

1933: the first concentration camps were like detention centres where opponents of the Nazis were sent to do forced labour. This photos shows Dachau concentration camp with its barracks and ammunition factory where Jews were sent to work for the German war effort. In many of the camps Jews were sometimes forced to take part in medical experiments by German doctors.

8

The Nazis herded the Jews together to live in ghettos – Jewish-only areas in the poorest slums, where they suffered from disease and hunger. Here, in 1941, in the Warsaw ghetto in Poland, Jews walk past the bodies of others who have starved to death. In the background is the wall that separated the ghetto from the rest of the city.

9

In this photograph taken at the concentration camp at Weimar, Germany when it was captured by the US Army on 14 April 1945, the bones of prisoners still lie in the crematoria.

10

The photo shows the building where the Wannsee Conference was held. Here, a group of top Nazi officials planned the systematic destruction of millions of Jews in Nazi-occupied countries across Europe in 1942. This plan was known as the Final Solution.

11

1942: the photo shows Nazi death squads carrying out an execution. Many shootings like this took place in Russia and Eastern Europe as part of the Final Solution but it was too slow and so death camps like Auschwitz were used to speed up the killing of the Jews across Europe.

GET ACTIVE 4

a Look at photos 1 to 11 and then put them in chronological order.
b How did each of the events shown in the photos change the everyday life of Jews?
c How did these events encourage ordinary Germans to see the Jews as inferior and treat them differently?
d The Jews were not the only group the Nazis persecuted. Use the internet to find out what the Nazis did to the gypsies, homosexuals, deaf people, and people with mental and physical disabilities.

HOW COULD THE HOLOCAUST HAVE HAPPENED?

The Holocaust was the result of a gradual process. This was supported, financed, planned, organised and carried out by the Nazi government. There were a number of steps to the Holocaust, each one leading into the next, as shown in the diagram below. It began with the persecution of Jews and other targeted minorities whom the Nazis regarded as racially inferior. It ended with the mass murder of Jews in death camps such as Auschwitz–Birkenau in Poland.

Descent to Annihilation

CREATE
Used propaganda to persuade people that Jews are the enemy and are subhuman so they deserve to be discriminated against. This is known as stereotyping.

CONTROL
Intimidated and threatened the German people with force or imprisonment in concentration camps if they did not accept these ideas and policies.

ISOLATE
Herded the Jews into ghettos or their own areas away from the rest of the population. Deported them to camps where many were worked to death.

ANNIHILATE
Produced specific plans in order to exterminate Jews on a large scale.

SOURCE 1

An extract from a book written in 1955 by Milton Mayer, an American college professor who researched how ordinary people reacted to Hitler's policies and ideas.

Small steps

If the last and worst act of the whole [Nazi] regime had come immediately after the first and smallest act, thousands, yes millions would have been sufficiently shocked – if, for example, the gassing of the Jews in 1943 had come immediately after the Jewish boycott in 1933. No, this is not the way it happens. In between come all the hundreds of little steps, some of them unnoticeable, each of them preparing you not to be too shocked by the next step. Step 3 is not so much worse than step 2 and if you didn't make a stand at step 2 why should you at step 3? And soon to step 4.

GET ACTIVE 5

a Study photos 2 to 5 on page 45. With a partner, match each photo to the description on each of the four steps of the staircase. Justify your choices. (You could then do the same for the photos on pages 44–5.)

b A stereotype is an image, word or phrase that reflects ideas that groups of people have about others who are different from them. Look at Source 2 on page 47. How does the author of the source stereotype the Jews? How would these stereotypes have helped the Nazis to persuade people that the Jews were their enemy?

c Study Source 1 on this page. What does it tell you about how the Holocaust happened?

SOURCE 2

A page from a Nazi story about the Jews for children, called The Poisonous Mushroom. *It was published in 1938 in a Nazi newspaper called* Der Sturmer.

SOURCE 3

A modern photo showing the railway lines at Birkenau extermination camp.

SOURCE 4

SS Chief Reinhard Heydrich who in 1942 organised a meeting of top-ranking Nazi officials in Wannsee, Berlin, to plan for the Final Solution to the Jewish question.

SOURCE 5

Death camps were set up all over Europe where Jews could be annihilated quickly on a mass scale. The photo shows Auschwitz–Birkenau where Zyklon B gas was used to exterminate Jews wholesale before their bodies were sent to crematoria.

A famous 'rescuer' was Oscar Schindler, who went to Poland to make money, but ended up giving his fortune to save his Jewish workers. His story is told in the film, *Schindler's List*. When asked why he did it, he said: 'When you know people, you have to behave toward them like human beings.'

HUMAN BEHAVIOUR AND THE HOLOCAUST

Historians of the Holocaust have classified human behaviour during the Nazi period in Germany into four categories:

PERPETRATORS (people who chose to participate in the Holocaust)	BYSTANDERS (people who did nothing)
VICTIMS (people who had no choice and had to do what they were told)	RESCUERS (people who helped the Jews)

SOURCE 1

A commandant's view

In a 1971 interview, journalist Gitta Sereny asked Franz Stangl, a Nazi death camp commandant: 'Didn't you feel that the Jews were human beings?' ...

'A cargo,' he said tonelessly. 'They were cargo ... I remember Christian Wirth [the man who set up the death camps] standing there in Treblinka next to the pits full of blue-black corpses. It was a mass of rotting flesh. He said "What shall we do with this garbage?" I think that started me thinking of them as cargo.'

SOURCE 2

The courage of Le Chambon

The people of Le Chambon, a small mountain village in France, knew that Jews were being murdered. Led by their pastor, Andre Trocine, they turned their community into a hiding place for 5,000 Jewish children from all over Europe. Andre's wife, Magda Trocine, said:

Those of us who received the first Jews did what we thought had to be done – nothing more complicated. It was not decided from one day to the next what we would have to do. There were many people in the village who needed help. How could we refuse them?

SOURCE 3

Arrival at Auschwitz

Leo Schneiderman, in an 1990 interview for the United States Holocaust Memorial Museum, describes his arrival at Auschwitz, the selection process, and how he was separated from his family:

It was late at night that we arrived at Auschwitz. When we came in, the minute the gates opened up, we heard screams, barking of dogs, blows from ... from those Kapos, those officials working for them, over the head. And then we got out of the train. And everything went so fast: left, right, right, left. Men separated from women. Children torn from the arms of mothers. The elderly chased like cattle. The sick, the disabled were handled like packs of garbage. They were thrown in a side together with broken suitcases, with boxes. My mother ran over to me and grabbed me by the shoulders, and she told me 'Leibele, I'm not going to see you no more. Take care of your brother.'

The bystanders

We are bystanders because we are ignorant, helpless and afraid.	Some state institutions like universities, and leaders of churches and schools, found it safer to say nothing.	By speaking out I could have placed the lives of my family and my neighbours in danger.
We believed what the government told us about the Jews.	I dare not help the Jews – I would get beaten up.	We can't help the Jews because it would be against the law.
The Jews are different to us so why should we help them?	We were brainwashed by Nazi propaganda into believing that Jews were inferior and dangerous to our country.	It is nothing to do with us.

Holocaust denial

Some scholars and right-wing political groups deny that the Holocaust happened. They argue that the existing pictures of Holocaust victims show only the acts of a few Nazi commanders at the end of the war, and that there was no formal 'genocide'. No written order from Hitler has been found, and they claim that the crematoria were too small to burn the bodies of millions of victims.

To accept these ideas requires us to believe that the thousands of Holocaust survivors are being untruthful about their experiences and to reject all the other evidence about the Holocaust.

Why is the Holocaust a significant event in the twentieth century?

- The Holocaust affected the lives of many people in the past.
- Things would have been different if this event had not happened – for example, we would not have the international recognition of Crimes Against Humanity.
- The Holocaust helps us to explain some things like other genocides or atrocities that exist in our world today.
- The Holocaust has affected the lives of survivors and their families now and for a long time to come.
- The study of the Holocaust can teach us valuable lessons about why and how people acted the way they did in the past.

GET ACTIVE 6

a Identify on pages 42–47 examples of perpetrators, bystanders, rescuers and victims. Write a few sentences explaining why each group acted as they did.

b Many ordinary Germans have been accused of bystander behaviour (see table on this page) and blamed for helping to cause the Holocaust. Make a list of arguments for and against this accusation.

c After the war some of the perpetrators were put on trial as war criminals. Use the internet to find out about the Nuremburg Trials in 1946. Do you think it is important that these crimes are recognised in this way?

The Jews

Until recently, many accounts of the Holocaust presented Jews only as the victims. We realise now that this view is not correct. Jewish reaction to the Holocaust included every type of reaction – from despair to proudly going to their death, and from armed resistance to collaboration with the Nazis.

Many Jews who could afford to do so fled abroad, many to the UK or America. These Jewish refugees are docking at Newcastle Quay, October 1939.

Many Jews arranged to send their children to foster parents abroad (this was known as Kindertransport). Between 1939 and 1948, nearly 300 Jewish children were saved because they passed through Magill's farm in Millisle, County Down, as part of the Kindertransport.

Some Jews delayed death by working for the Nazis. The photo shows Jewish men who were members of a 'Sonderkommando' unit. In October 1944 one of these Sonderkommando units revolted in Auschwitz and destroyed one of the crematoria as well as killing three SS guards.

Hearing they were to be sent to death camps, in January 1943 the Jews in the Warsaw ghetto disappeared into hiding places, and then fought off the German army for nearly a month – an heroic resistance in the face of impossible odds. This Jewish fighter is surrendering on 9 May, the 21st day of the uprising.

Dutch Jews leave for 'resettlement' in a concentration camp, 1942. The Jewish Council has organised their departure, and they have paid for their tickets.

GET ACTIVE 7

a Identify the different ways that the Jews on this page reacted to the Holocaust.
b Looking back at pages 44–48, what other ways can you see Jewish people reacting?
c Explain why these photos are important when studying how Jews behaved during the Holocaust.

Plan, Do, Review

This chapter has looked at the Holocaust, why and how it happened, and how people reacted to it at the time. In this section we will focus on your own reactions to the Holocaust by looking at the ways in which it has been remembered today.

Your Principal has asked you to design and plan your own Holocaust Memorial Day to represent the school's contribution to the international commemoration which takes place on 27 January each year. Your task will be to present your form of commemoration to your Principal and the whole school at assembly, or to your class.

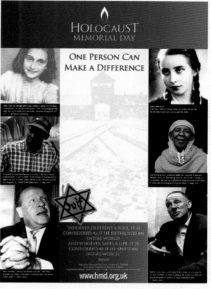

This is the poster from the 2006 Holocaust Memorial Day.

PLAN

1   Go back through the chapter and collect information about what happened. You may also wish to visit these websites:
www.hmd.org.uk
www.het.org.uk
www.ushmm.org
www.hetireland.org
Use examples of primary evidence as well as other information.
2   Discuss with a group of other pupils the form your memorial will take – for instance, you may decide to include a poster, stories and facts about the Holocaust, witness statements from victims of the Holocaust, poetry, artwork, readings, or even a formal memorial, such as a shrine.
3   Decide:
   ● Who will be the audience?
   ● What will your key messages be?
   ● How can your form of commemoration show sufficient respect to the occasion, and is it sensitive to the seriousness of the topic?

DO

1   Working individually, or in groups, prepare your memorial.
2   Take proper account of the quantity and quality of your materials, and keep to deadlines.
3   Present your memorial to the class or in assembly.

REVIEW

1   Which form of commemoration did you find the most interesting and why? How was it different to yours? Is there anything about your own commemoration that you would do differently the next time?
2   Discuss as a class why you think we should study the Holocaust in schools today and why it is a significant event of the twentieth century.

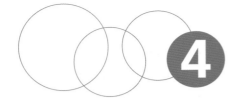

4 Significant events and individuals – what and who made a difference in the twentieth century?

In this chapter we are learning to:
- ✓ make judgements about what makes an event or person significant;
- ✓ further develop decision-making skills through an examination of significant events and individuals in the twentieth century;
- ✓ investigate the motivation of individuals and governments;
- ✓ demonstrate self-management and enquiry skills through a personal and group investigation.

GET ACTIVE 1

a All the events shown on this page were memorable, but were they 'significant' events? Talk to people in your family or community who remember these events and ask them why they think they were significant.

b Make a list in a discussion group of some of the big events you can remember happening in your lifetime. Do you consider any of them to have been 'significant' moments in history? Why?

c 'You can only really tell whether an event was historically significant hundreds of years after.' Do you agree? Look back at the list of criteria which make an event 'significant' (page 18). Suggest reasons why you need to wait many years before you can declare an event 'historically significant'.

SECTION ONE – SIGNIFICANT EVENTS

What makes an event significant?

Royal wedding of Prince Charles and Princess Diana, 29 July 1981.

Release of Nelson Mandela, 11 February 1990. People all over the world had campaigned for his release and the end of apartheid in South Africa.

Terrorist attack on New York's Twin Towers, 11 September 2001.

Liverpool winning the Champions League, 25 May 2005.

A SIGNIFICANT EVENT – THE WALL COMES DOWN

In November 1989 thousands of Germans went to a big wall that ran through the centre of Berlin. They stood on it and climbed over it. They attacked it with pickaxes, sledgehammers and even chisels. They laughed and cried and cheered. Men in big diggers pushed it over. Others gathered lumps of the concrete and sold them as souvenirs.

The fall of the Berlin Wall in 1989 was one of the historically significant events of the twentieth century. In itself it may seem a small thing – it was just a wall, and it proved physically easy to knock it down. Hardly anything remains of it today.

Why should knocking down a wall cause so much joy?

The first section of this chapter will consider why this is so.

Celebrating the fall of the Berlin Wall.

GET ACTIVE 2

a 'The fall of the Berlin Wall in 1989 WAS historically significant.' Explain in your own words what *you think* this actually *means*.

b 'Why should knocking down a wall cause so much joy?' In your discussion groups, make a list of questions you would like to ask to 'get to the bottom' of this – on the face of it – surprising event. (Use the images on this page to help you.)

c When you have thought of a list of questions, share them together as a whole class. As you go through the story of the Berlin Wall look out for the brick ✉ symbol and check off your questions as they are answered.

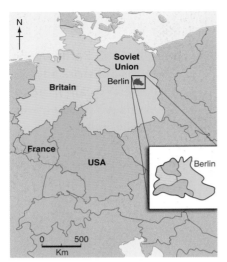

Map showing the parts of Germany occupied by the four Allied forces at the end of the Second World War.

In 1946, the British leader Winston Churchill warned the west that an 'Iron Curtain' had come down between the free west and the Soviet Bloc. ✉
'The Communist parties ... are seeking everywhere to obtain totalitarian control,' he warned. The Soviet government said that his speech was a declaration of war.

This cartoon by a Russian artist is dated 1947. Churchill is shown as a war-maker, following in the footsteps of Hitler and the Nazis.

HOW DID THE WALL COME TO BE BUILT?

In 1945, after the defeat of Hitler, the victorious allies each occupied a different zone of Germany (see map). Berlin, although it was deep inside the Soviet sector, was also divided into four sectors. This meant that the British, American and French controlled territory deep inside the Soviet zone. ✉ What made this a problem was that the post-war world was not united. There were deep divisions between the USSR – 'the Soviets' – and the western allies (Britain, France and the USA). ✉ The USSR was a Communist country and society; the western allies were DEMOCRACIES. Their differences are shown in the table below.

USA	USSR
Choice of political parties.	Only one party allowed.
Freedom of speech.	Media strictly controlled by the government.
Citizens free to make as much money as they can.	Economy controlled for the good of the state.
Class system – extremes of rich and poor.	Equality – less difference between rich and poor.
Fierce belief that their way of life is right.	Fierce belief that their way of life is right.

It wasn't long before the clash of beliefs had developed into open conflict. The USSR occupied the countries of eastern Europe it had 'liberated' at the end of the Second World War, and made sure that hard-line pro-Soviet Communist governments took power there. ✉ Fearful of this growing Soviet influence, the USA poured billions of dollars of 'MARSHALL AID' into Europe – which was seen by the Soviets simply as 'dollar IMPERIALISM' (buying an empire). ✉

By 1948, the west and the Soviets had become enemies. They could not, however, actually GO to war. Both sides were too afraid to use the most powerful bomb in history – the atomic bomb. To go to war would be MAD ('Mutually Assured Destruction'). They would destroy the world. So they had a 'Cold War' instead; they did everything they could to destroy their enemy short of actually fighting.

GET ACTIVE 3

a Look at a map of Europe. Why might the Soviets have wanted to *control* the countries of eastern Europe? What might the USA *gain* from providing aid to post-war Europe?
b Study Source 1 and the information on this page to explain why both sides *distrusted* each other and why war *didn't* break out in 1948.

The Berlin Blockade, 1948

Berlin had already been the centre of one crisis in 1948.
Trying to stimulate the German economy, on 23 June 1948, the western allies introduced a new currency (money) into their zones. Since the western economies were much stronger than the Soviet economy, everybody in the Soviet zone wanted the new money. There was a run on the banks in the Soviet zone. So, on 24 June 1948 the Soviet leader Stalin closed the borders with the western sectors of Berlin.

The western allies interpreted this as an attempt by Stalin to conquer West Berlin by starving it into surrender. Berlin became a symbol of the Cold War. For eleven months the allies supplied West Berlin by air. When Stalin called off the BLOCKADE on 12 May 1949, the British and Americans said they had saved West Berlin.

The Berlin airlift

The Berlin Wall, 1961

In the years after 1948, Berlin became an embarrassment to the Soviets. West Berlin was so much more prosperous than East Berlin that it made the Communist way of life look bad.
Many East Berliners worked in West Berlin; by 1961, every day 2,000 East Germans (many of them skilled workers) went into West Berlin and escaped from there to the west. Besides which, the Soviet government believed that the Americans were using Berlin as a spy base.

In June 1961, the Soviet leader Khrushchev demanded that the Americans leave Berlin. When the American President John F. Kennedy refused, Berliners woke up on the morning of 13 August 1961 to discover that the East German government had built a wall across the middle of Berlin.

SOURCE 2

The wall prevented imperialism from contaminating the east ... Moreover, people of East Germany were not 'walled in'! They could go to Poland or Hungary. They just couldn't go to western countries. Because, naturally, you don't travel around in enemy territory.

Von Schnitzler, former presenter on East German TV, interviewed in the 1990s. Schnitzler's job had been to counter the 'corrupting influence' of western TV on East German people.

GET ACTIVE 4

a Study Source 2. Is it a biased source? Explain your answer.
b Many factors contributed to the Wall being built. How many factors can you find on pages 54–55? Some have been marked with a brick symbol – – but can you spot any more?
c Draw some bricks, write each factor onto each of them, and stick them on a pin-board, in date order. Taking each one in turn, try to explain *how* that factor helped to cause the building of the Berlin Wall.

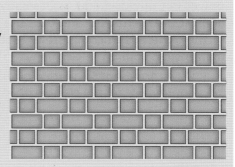

SOURCE 1

There are many people in the world who really don't understand what is the great issue between the free world and the Communist world.

Let them come to Berlin! There are some who say in Europe and elsewhere we can work with the Communists.

Let them come to Berlin!

From a speech by American President Kennedy, in Berlin, in 1963. Kennedy spoke next to the wall, and made sure that he could be heard on the other side of the wall, where East Germans had gathered to listen.

SOURCE 2

'Why do you have to have the wall?' one of the tourists asked. They listened as the officer explained to them what the situation was before August 13th, 1961.

The officer said: 'Since 1961 we have been able to build up socialism more effectively than ever before. West Berlin has often been misused as a centre of attacks against our Republic. But the imperialists won't get through our frontier!'

From English For You, an East German school textbook (1979).

SOURCE 3

It all worked without a hitch! The measures to ensure peace caught our enemies entirely by surprise. ... A power has developed in Germany that can stand against barbaric militarism ... The militarists suffered a defeat! The balance of power in the world and in Germany has turned against the militarists, and thus the beginning of the general and complete defeat of the militarists is coming in Germany!

Argument 55, written by the East German government for the election of September 1961.

1961: East German parents hold up their babies for the children's grandparents, who live in West Berlin, to see. The grandparents would never be able to hold their grandchildren, and soon even these meetings were stopped.

LIVING WITH THE WALL

Life on the two sides of the Berlin Wall was very different. West Germany became one of the most prosperous countries in Europe. Life for people in East Germany was harder, but many supported the Communist system and saw it as providing a fairer distribution of wealth. Many were proud of its education system and the honours won by its sportsmen at the Olympics. However, few dared to oppose the Communist government, which kept control through a secret police force called the Stasi. Anyone who was suspected of disloyalty against the state could be punished or removed from their job.

Over the years, the Wall was strengthened and improved. It became a symbol of the Cold War. It divided Berlin, but it was a symbol of the division between the USSR and the Eastern Bloc countries under its control and the USA and the western democracies. Each side used it as a PROPAGANDA weapon against the other.

SOURCE 4

Despite great danger, many people did try to escape to the west. Between 1961–1989, 171 people were killed and many more seriously wounded trying to cross the heavily guarded wall. Many more were arrested and imprisoned.

On 17 August 1962, an East German teenager, Peter Fechter, was wounded in the back, shot by East German guards while trying to escape. He lay in a barbed wire fence, slowly bleeding to death, in full view of the world's media. American soldiers could not rescue him because he was a few yards inside the Soviet sector. East German border guards were reluctant to approach him for fear of provoking western soldiers, one of whom had shot an East German border guard just days earlier. Eventually his body was removed by the East German guards.

SOURCE 5

The Spy Who Came In From The Cold (1965) was an angry film about the Cold War. In the story, neither side is any longer fighting for anything decent. The star of the film was the Wall and the sense of doom and tension it created. The story ends as the embittered hero tries to pull his idealistic young Communist girlfriend over the Wall to freedom. She is shot and killed, and he climbs back down, to be shot and killed also.

GET ACTIVE 5

a Study Source 1. Explain what President Kennedy is saying about the wall.

b Study Sources 2 and 3. List all the arguments that the Communists used to justify the Wall.

c Do an internet search on 'Berlin Wall escape attempts' and make notes on the different ways East Germans tried to escape to the west.

d Use the information on page 56 and Sources 4 and 5 to explain why people in East Berlin might have wanted to escape over the Wall.

THE SOVIET UNION AND EASTERN EUROPE /-
IF YOU SEEK LIBERALIZATION, COME HERE,
TO THIS GATE.

MR. GORBACHEV, OPEN THIS GATE.

MR. GORBACHEV, TEAR DOWN THIS WALL.

I UNDERSTAND THE FEAR OF WAR AND THE
PAIN OF DIVISION THAT AFFLICT THIS
CONTINENT /- AND I PLEDGE TO YOU MY
COUNTRY'S EFFORTS TO HELP OVERCOME THESE

On 12 June 1987, President Reagan of the USA visited Berlin and appealed to Gorbachev to tear down the Berlin Wall and end the Cold War. This is the speech card from which he spoke.

THE WALL COMES DOWN

In 1985 Mikhail Gorbachev became leader of the SOVIET UNION. He inherited a country with many problems. The cost of the Soviet armed forces had ruined the economy and the countryside was polluted with industrial waste. Chernobyl, the world's worst nuclear-power disaster, had exposed the failure of Soviet industry. Russian troops were fighting a losing and costly war in Afghanistan. In 1987, the American President, Ronald Reagan, who had been pouring money into the ARMS RACE with the USSR, came to West Berlin to urge the new Russian President to tear down the wall.

Gorbachev decided that things had to change and began to introduce both economic and political reforms in Russia. His policies of *PERESTROIKA* (reform), and *GLASNOST* (openness) led people to dare to challenge the Communist system and its belief in absolute control.

Gorbachev also began DISARMAMENT talks with the American President. In 1987 the two presidents agreed to end the arms race and to destroy some of their atomic weapons. The Cold War was beginning to thaw. Gorbachev declared that the Soviet Union would no longer interfere in the affairs of the Iron Curtain countries.

Many people in Hungary, Poland, Czechoslovakia and Romania were encouraged by what was happening in Russia. They felt brave enough to march on the streets demanding free elections. People in the west watched with amazement and delight at these peaceful mass demonstrations. Could the old Communist governments of eastern Europe really be coming to an end? In the spring of 1989, young students in China, inspired by what was happening in Europe, challenged their Communist leaders. On 3 June, people all over the world watched in horror as tanks rolled into Tiananmen Square and opened fire on unarmed protestors.

The people of East and West Germany could see what was happening in other countries. On 9 November 1989 thousands of East Berliners marched on the Berlin Wall and demanded entry to the west. The guards were swamped and didn't know what to do. After a tense moment, the guards let them through. In the following days, crowds of East and West Berliners came with pickaxes and hammers and broke down the Wall.

Across eastern Europe the Communist governments of Romania, Czechoslovakia, Poland and Hungary were besieged by armies of protestors and forced to resign. 1989 had proved to be a decisive year, bringing the end of communism and dramatic political changes across Eastern Europe.

SOURCE 1

When we knew that Gorbachev was thinking about reform, we saw he would not oppose our reforms, and that was important to us.

From an interview with Lech Walesa, leader of the Solidarity reform movement in Poland.

SOURCE 2

Gorbachev gave us great hope. He tried to change his country in the same way as we wanted to change our country – through *perestroika*, a gradual liberalisation.

From an interview with Stefan Heym, an East German writer.

SOURCE 3

If you live in a system that is oppressive, you don't walk upright, you always go with your head down, and now was a chance to walk upright and to show your face and to show the power of the people.

From an interview with Monika Langeman, a resident of East Berlin.

After the fall of the Wall

Within a year, the East and West parts of Germany were united. It was very difficult uniting two very different political, social and economic systems. While many in the East enjoyed their new political freedoms, others found it hard to adjust to making their own decisions for the first time in their lives. Wages, rent and prices had all been lower in the East and unification brought financial hardship and competition for jobs and university places. Some West Germans began to resent the huge amount of money that was now invested into the former East Germany.

The collapse of the Wall hastened the collapse of the Soviet Union in 1991. All the countries of eastern Europe who had been controlled by the Soviet Union were free and began to hold democratic elections. Many sought to join the European Union (EU). One result of this was the opening up of all Europe to workers and tourists. Citizens of the EU have the same rights and privileges, and workers from Ireland, Portugal, Poland and other member countries have migrated to find work.

Economically, the fall of the Wall also brought capitalism to the former Eastern Bloc countries. Some became very rich, like Roman Abramovich, who used some of his fortune to buy Chelsea Football Club. Financial markets became more global, impacting on countries all over the world.

The post-1989 world is all about change and, internationally, we live in uncertain times.

SOURCE 4

I found myself in a group of people who were clapping. I didn't understand why. Then I realised. I was in West Berlin, and West Berliners had come to the border and they were clapping us. We were all crying and hugging each other.

Monika Langeman recalls her first visit to West Berlin. The West German government gave every visitor from East Germany some money and let them go shopping in West Berlin.

SOURCE 5

You had to be there to feel the true significance of the event. I truly feel blessed to have lived through that moment with all the other citizens of Berlin, both East and West. It is a moment I will never forget.

Luann Brennan, writing about the fall of the Berlin Wall.

SOURCE 6

Why, now that it's breached, broken, does it
  cause such consternation in me? ...
The past is a prison I long for ...
and something in my old heart
  wants to ... retain ...
  the orderly street, the fading State
  offices, [and]
knowing myself to be a good citizen, inspected
  therefore respected, and that the State ...
  would protect me from death.

The Berlin Wall was published in 2003 by the Canadian poet George Stanley (born 1934). The poet has mixed feelings about the unknown new world opened up by the fall of the Berlin Wall, and looks back fondly on the old certainties.

GET ACTIVE 6

a Using the information on page 56, find FIVE reasons for the fall of the Wall.
b Using the information on page 57, find FIVE results of the fall of the Wall.
c Look at Sources 1 and 2. What view is given about the role of Gorbachev in the fall of the Berlin Wall?
d Compare Sources 3 and 6. How do the views of the two writers differ? Suggest reasons why they have these different views of life behind the Wall.
e Was the fall of the Berlin Wall a significant event? Once again, use the six criteria you learned on page 16 to help you make a decision.

SECTION TWO – SIGNIFICANT PEOPLE

Throughout history ordinary people have made their mark. Some are heroes standing bravely against tyranny and cruelty. Some are innovators who change the way we think, work or look at things. Some are sportsmen or artists who inspire others to be the best they can in their field.

Remember: being significant is not the same as being famous!

- If people are famous it means that lots of people have heard of them.
- If people are significant it means that they have done things that affected other people's lives in important ways (for good or bad) – although you may not have heard of them.

The following pages examine the lives of two famous people from the twentieth century to see if *they* were 'significant' individuals.

Emmeline Pankhurst

Story

Emmeline Pankhurst was born in Manchester in the middle of the nineteenth century, at a time when women could not vote and had few legal rights. She was lucky in having parents who believed in the importance of education for women and they encouraged her to think for herself. She married a wealthy lawyer and could have chosen to live the life expected by society at that time, as mistress of a household of servants. Instead, she became a Poor Law Guardian, visiting the local workhouse.

Emmeline was horrified at how society treated women and decided that only when women had the vote would there be laws making their lives better. When her husband died suddenly in 1898, Emmeline and her daughters, Christabel and Sylvia, became more involved in the campaign for the vote. They founded a new organisation called the Women's Social and Political Union (WSPU) and urged members to use MILITANT tactics to gain women's SUFFRAGE (the vote).

At that time, many women (called 'Suffragists') were campaigning for the vote, but they did so peacefully, presenting petitions and holding meetings. Emmeline's 'Suffragettes', as they became known, shouted out in Parliament, organised marches, chained themselves to railings and broke windows. 'We are not here because we are law breakers,' Emmeline asserted. 'We are here in our efforts to become law *makers*.'

Emmeline Pankhurst was commemorated in the 1964 movie *Mary Poppins,* where Mrs Banks (a fanatical Suffragette) sings: 'Mrs Pankhurst has been clapped in irons again.'

As time went on, the Suffragettes' campaign became more violent. They burned down churches and stately homes. When they were arrested, the Suffragettes claimed they were political prisoners and not ordinary criminals. They went on hunger strike and were forcibly fed. Emmeline and her daughters encouraged their followers to make even more daring protests and, in 1913, one suffragette, Emily Davison, was killed when she tried to grab the King's horse in the Derby horse race.

Emmeline made a number of speaking visits to Ireland, but was not well-received by the Irish Suffragists, who felt she was trying to take over their movement.

When the First World War broke out in August 1914, Emmeline and her eldest daughter supported the war effort. The WSPU announced it was suspending its campaign, even though 'Votes for Women' had not been granted, and marched with banners with slogans such as 'We Demand the Right to Serve' and 'Men must fight and women must work'.

In 1930, a statue of Emmeline Pankhurst was erected by public subscription near the Houses of Parliament. In April 1979, it was visited by Margaret Thatcher, shortly before she became Britain's first woman Prime Minister.

Judgement

When the war ended, the government awarded all women over the age of 30 the right to vote. But was this as a result of what Emmeline Pankhurst had done? Some historians have pointed out that, when the Suffragettes suspended their campaign in 1914, they had failed to win the vote for women. They say that Emmeline's militant tactics actually turned people against the cause and that it was the patriotic work women did during the war, and the peaceful persuasion of the Suffragists, which won the vote for women in the end. Other historians, however, say that by forcefully demanding the vote, and by challenging the traditional roles of wives, mothers and daughters, Emmeline made women's rights public, and paved the way for the feminist and women's liberation movements of the 1960s and 70s.

Emmeline stood for Parliament, but failed to win a seat. She died in 1928.

GET ACTIVE 7

a Use pages 60–61 to make notes on Emmeline Pankhurst. Pick out things where she might be praised for her achievements or criticised for her faults.

b Carry out an internet search to find out more information about Emmeline Pankhurst.

c Read about Bill Gates on the next page and repeat the same enquiry.

Bill Gates speaking at a conference on the internet. He says: 'Back when I was a teenager, I envisioned the impact that low-cost computers could have. A computer on every desk and in every home.'

BILL GATES

Story

Bill Gates was born in 1955 in Seattle, Washington, USA, to very wealthy parents. He attended private schools and was a good student. He became interested in computers at a time when they were huge mainframe machines used only by specially-trained technicians. He was especially interested in developing software for computers and when only 15 years old he wrote his school's timetabling program (coding it so that he was placed in classes with mostly girls!). Later, he dropped out of Harvard University to start a computer software company.

Judgement

It is arguable that no one in the twentieth century has had as much impact as Bill Gates on how men and women live and work. Every day, millions of families, office workers, doctors, administrators and teachers use products such as Microsoft Word. Meanwhile, Internet Explorer keeps the world in touch on the internet – in 2006, users worldwide spent 21 billion hours on the internet; 80 per cent of them used Internet Explorer.

Bill Gates became one of the richest men in the world but he felt he had a responsibility to do good things with his wealth. He studied the work of other American PHILANTHROPISTS such as Andrew Carnegie and John D. Rockefeller and in 1994 he created the W.H. Gates Foundation. The Foundation has given billions of pounds to trying to solve many of the world's problems, such as hunger, the prevention of disease, and healthcare and education for all.

SOURCE 1

Criteria for establishing the significance of an individual

- Created something new.
- Became famous in his/her own lifetime.
- Actively supported good causes.
- Was a great leader.
- Fought to free people from bad government or unjust laws.
- Saved people's lives.
- Changed people's lives for the better.
- Worked very hard.
- Had a wide range of interests.
- Made a fortune.

Suggested by a history teacher.

GET ACTIVE 8

a Do the 'Criteria of significance' for an event (page 18) also apply to people?

b A teacher colleague has suggested some additional criteria (Source 1). What do you think of her ideas?

c Working with a partner, draw up your own list of: 'Criteria for establishing the significance of an individual'. Use them to decide whether Emmeline Pankhurst or Bill Gates are 'significant' characters in history.

d In 2002, the BBC held a competition to find the *100 Greatest Britons.* Use the internet to find out who won.

Plan, Do, Review

SIGNIFICANT EVENTS AND INDIVIDUALS

In this chapter you have studied one event and two individuals and considered their significance. In this **Plan, Do, Review** exercise, you will use the skills you have learned to debate and choose your own 'most significant' event or individual.

PLAN

Stage 1

Divide into groups. Each group needs to decide whether to study events OR individuals:

- agree how you will vote for your choice – e.g. first-past-the-post, single transferable vote, etc.;
- design an application form, similar to the one on this page, on which each member of the group can submit their choice;
- each group member prepares to champion their candidate;
- listen to each other. Be prepared to defend your choice but also learn why others think their choice is better. You will need to reach a consensus;
- respect the group's choice;
- make sure each group has chosen a different event or person. Some groups may have to re-think their choice.

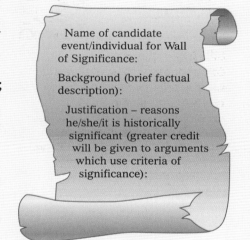

Name of candidate event/individual for Wall of Significance:

Background (brief factual description):

Justification – reasons he/she/it is historically significant (greater credit will be given to arguments which use criteria of significance):

DO

Agree a time deadline for the presentations. Help your group to:

- research the chosen event or person, concentrating on reasons he/she/it was significant;
- think about whether the event or person had a political, social, economic, cultural or technological impact;
- prepare a short presentation with words and images championing your choice.

Hold a balloon debate

Appoint a class chairperson to manage proceedings, each group taking turns to present their candidate. Make sure your presentations keep to the agreed time deadline.

Use the chosen method of deciding who should stay in the balloon and be featured on the class Wall of Significance.

REVIEW

Reflect on the activity, and **your role** in this task. **Ask:** *What did I do well? Did I use my research skills effectively? Did I present information clearly and ask good questions? Was I a good group member? Did I help my group reach an agreement?*

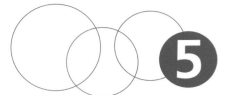

5 Why was Ireland partitioned?

In this chapter we are learning to:
- ✓ analyse and explain the causes of partition;
- ✓ understand why partition is still important today;
- ✓ write your own explanation about why Ireland was partitioned.

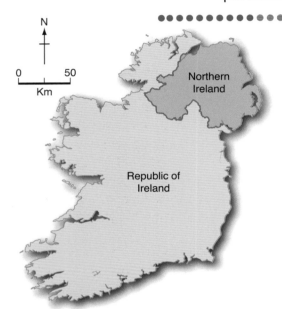

N

0   50
Km

Northern Ireland

Republic of Ireland

A map of Ireland today showing how Ireland was divided politically in 1921.

Today, Ireland is divided politically into two states – the six counties of Northern Ireland and the 26 counties of the Republic of Ireland. This division came about in 1921 when Ireland was partitioned. In the next two chapters we will investigate the causes and consequences of partition in 1921 and how significant a part it played in the SECTARIAN violence in Northern Ireland known as 'the Troubles'.

We will think about the causes of partition and consider if there were any alternative political solutions to end the conflict in Ireland.

GET ACTIVE 1

a Look at both wall murals in Sources 1 and 2. Think about which one you would describe as NATIONALIST and which one as UNIONIST.

b Share your ideas with a partner and look for words, symbols or designs that are similar or different.

c Now share your ideas with the rest of the class. What did you agree and disagree on?

SOURCE 1

Wall mural in West Belfast, painted in 1991.

SOURCE 2

Wall mural on the Newtownards Road, Belfast, painted in 1992.

PARTITION – WHAT HAPPENED AND WHEN?

Some historians trace the causes of partition over hundreds of years. Others say the causes took place in the period 1900–1921 with the struggle over HOME RULE. On pages 66–7 we will examine these longer-term causes of the partition of Ireland, but first let's look at an overview of the key events you will be investigating throughout the chapter.

1921 The Anglo–Irish Treaty. The 26 southern counties became the Irish Free State; the six northern counties remained part of the United Kingdom.

1919–1921 The War of Independence between Republicans and British forces, called the Black and Tans.

1918 *Sinn Féin* won 73 seats out of 105 in the election. They set up a parliament (the Dail) in Dublin.

1916 The Easter Rising in Dublin, when a group of Irish Nationalists failed in their attempts to get an independent Irish Republic.

1914 A Third Home Rule Bill was passed, but postponed because of the First World War.

1913 Both the ULSTER VOLUNTEER FORCE (UVF) and the IRISH VOLUNTEERS obtained supplies of illegal arms.

1912 Many Ulster Unionists signed a 'Solemn League and Covenant'.

1905 (March) Ulster Protestants formed the Ulster Unionist Council to oppose Home Rule. (November) Irish nationalists founded SINN FÉIN to campaign for independence.

1886–1893 Two Home Rule bills were defeated in Westminster.

1858 The IRISH REPUBLICAN BROTHERHOOD (the 'Fenians') were formed and organised a revolt to get independence for Ireland.

1845–1849 The Irish Famine.

1829 Catholic Emancipation – Catholics gained political and religious freedom.

1801 Act of Union – Ireland became part of the United Kingdom.

1798 UNITED IRISHMEN rebellion against Britain.

1690 Battle of the Boyne: William of Orange won. The Catholics were subjected to Penal Laws.

1649 Cromwell campaign in Ireland.

1610 The first Protestant Planters arrived in Ulster as part of the Plantation.

1172 Henry II conquered Ireland and made himself Lord of Ireland.

GET ACTIVE 2

a Read the events on the timeline out loud with a partner. Then write a list of events by classifying them into:
  i those events that would have interested Unionists;
  ii those events that would have interested Nationalists.
b Are there events that would have interested both Nationalists and Unionist?
c Which of the events on the timeline might have influenced Britain to tighten her control over Ireland?
d Chose one event from the timeline that a Unionist or Nationalist artist might represent in a wall mural. Share your ideas with the class.

HOME RULE FOR IRELAND

One event on the timeline that would have interested many people in Ireland in the late nineteenth century was the movement for Home Rule. Home Rule meant that Ireland would be able to rule her own internal affairs while Britain would keep control of foreign affairs. By the end of the chapter you will have considered how disagreements in Ireland over Home Rule would be one of the key causes of partition in 1921.

THE LONG-TERM CAUSES OF PARTITION

1 Independence for Ireland

For many centuries since the Norman invasion of Ireland in 1169 there had been attempts by different groups of people in Ireland to win independence from Britain. The panels below contain descriptions of the methods Britain used to prevent Ireland becoming independent and to maintain control.

1 1100s–1400s
The Normans, under Henry II and Strongbow, invaded Ireland in 1169 and took control of most of the island. However, by the fifteenth century their influence had shrunk to a small area around Dublin called the Pale. Most of Ireland had gone back to the control of the Irish, many of whom had intermarried with the original Anglo-Norman invaders.

2 1500s–1600s
Henry VIII started the English Reformation in 1534 by breaking away from the Roman Catholic Church and forming a new Church of England. In 1541 he changed his title from Lord to King of Ireland as a warning to Catholic countries in Europe not to use Ireland as a base to attack England. This was followed by a period during which England tried to keep control in Ireland by using the FIRST PLANTATIONS, but they were not successful. Eventually, Elizabeth I strengthened England's control over Ireland in a series of wars and campaigns.

3 1600s–1700s
In the seventeenth century England tightened her control over Ireland by extending the system of plantations. This time, a new plan was drawn up by which the English government encouraged English and Scottish protestants to settle in Ulster. The land came from the original landowners, who eventually rose up in rebellion in 1641. The rebellion was crushed by Cromwell in 1649. In 1690, the Protestant English King William of Orange defeated the Catholic King James II at the Battle of the Boyne, and this put Protestants firmly in control in Ulster.

4 1700s–1800s
While William of Orange was fighting in Europe he passed the Penal Laws to keep Catholics in Ireland under control. These laws restricted movements of Catholics and prevented them from having a gun, owning property, buying land or becoming an MP. These laws lasted until well into the nineteenth century. In 1798, the United Irishmen planned a rebellion to overthrow the British government with the help of France, but this revolt failed. The rebellion forced Britain to pass the Act of Union, which restored her control of Ireland by abolishing the Irish Parliament.

5 1800s–1900s
In 1829, Catholics were allowed to become MPs and the Penal Laws were relaxed. However, many Irish Catholics believed that they would not get better treatment or independence for Ireland by peaceful means, so they decided to use physical force. In 1867, a group belonging to the Irish Republican Brotherhood, and led by the FENIANS, revolted against the British government. Their rebellion was put down, however. After this, many Irishmen began to support the idea of Home Rule and in 1870 the Home Rule movement was formed. Home Rule for Ireland meant that Ireland would control her own affairs but the parliament at Westminster would still keep control over foreign affairs.

GET ACTIVE 3

Read the statements above. Match the number of each statement with one of the 'methods of control' boxes on page 67.

METHODS OF CONTROL

Restrictions and union

Invasion and conquest

Plantation

Control and consolidate

Home Rule bills

SOURCE 1

Extract from the Oath of the Orange Order. This organisation was founded in Ulster in 1795 at a time when there were frequent sectarian riots between Protestant and Catholic gangs.

I do solemnly and sincerely swear of my own free will ... that I will, to the utmost of my power, support and defend the present King George III and the crown so long as they support the PROTESTANT ASCENDANCY ... I do further swear that I am not nor ever was, a Roman Catholic or PAPIST; that I was not nor ever will be a United Irishman.

SOURCE 2

In 1798, Wolfe Tone (1763–1798) led a rebellion of the United Irishmen, composed of both Presbyterians and Catholics, in order to win independence for Ireland. Despite having the help of a French force and fleet the rebellion was put down and Wolfe Tone was captured and later took his own life in November 1798.

SOURCE 3

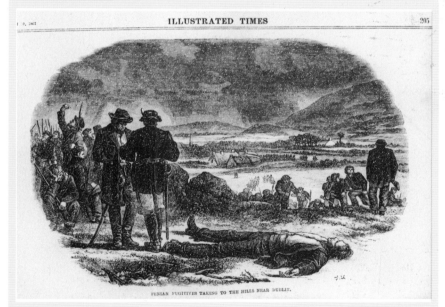

ILLUSTRATED TIMES
205

FENIAN FUGITIVES TAKING TO THE HILLS NEAR DUBLIN.

The Fenians were an organisation founded in America in 1858 to win independence for Ireland. Fenian in Irish means warrior. This cartoon shows the unsuccessful Fenian Rising in 1867. This revolt was supported by the Irish Republican Brotherhood, formed to win independence for Ireland through physical force.

GET ACTIVE 4

a Look at Sources 1 to 3. What do they tell you about who wanted independence for Ireland and who wanted to stay under British rule?

b What do the sources tell you about the methods used by the different groups?

2 Divided society

As you have seen in the last section, people in Ireland were divided by their attitudes and beliefs. Many of these ideas had been shaped by political events and are by no means simple to define. As well as having different political beliefs, people in Ireland were divided by long-standing ideas about their identity, sense of belonging and religion.

In Year 9 you learned about how the differences in religious identity had started with the Reformation in the sixteenth century when Catholics resented the restrictions on their form of worship and the privileges granted to members of the Church of England. You may also remember from Year 9 how the Plantation of Ulster in the early 1600s had reinforced these religious differences as well as adding to the feelings of alienation among Irish Catholics. The new Protestant settlers were suspicious of their Catholic neighbours whose land they had been given.

- We comprise three-quarters of the population of Ireland.
- We include tenant farmers and agricultural labourers.
- We are mainly Catholic.
- We like Gaelic games such as hurling and speak Gaelic.
- We believe that the Act of Union has ruined Ireland's prosperity.

- In the north of Ireland we make up two-thirds of the population.
- We include landowners, farmers, industrialists and factory workers.
- We are Protestant.
- We enjoy football.
- We believe that the Act of Union has allowed the growth of industries in Ulster, which has made us prosperous.

3 The failure of Home Rule

The divisions between Nationalists and Unionists became more intense over the proposals by the British government to grant Home Rule to Ireland. The first two attempts at passing Home Rule bills in 1886 and 1893 had failed and in 1912 it looked like the Third Home Rule bill would be passed.

In Westminster, the two main political parties were called the LIBERALS and the CONSERVATIVES. The Conservative Party opposed Home Rule because they thought it would lead to the break-up of the Empire, and because they feared an Irish parliament would pass laws to prevent English goods being sold in Ireland.

The Protestants of Ulster were even more opposed to Home Rule. They worried that an Irish parliament, which would be dominated by Catholics, would start to attack the Protestant religion – 'Home Rule is Rome Rule', the saying went. They feared that Ulster's linen and shipbuilding industries would be damaged by the break with England. Most of all, they just did not trust the Catholic majority to be able to rule Ireland properly.

GET ACTIVE 5

a Look at the diagram on page 68. Which of these two people would have been most likely to:
- have wanted to stay in the United Kingdom?
- have wanted Ireland to have Home Rule?
- have believed that Home Rule would ruin Ulster?
- have been a member of the Gaelic League?
- have marched to celebrate the Battle of the Boyne?
- have remembered the Famine with anger?

b Make a list of all the reasons the Unionists and Conservatives opposed Home Rule.

John Redmond
- Leader of Irish Parliamentary Party who supported Home Rule for Ireland.
- Most of his support came from Irish Catholics.
- By 1910 there were 82 Irish Parliamentary Party members in Westminster.

Edward Carson
- Leader of the Unionists.
- His main support came from the Protestant Orange Order in Ulster and the British Conservative Party in Britain.
- Under his leadership, opposition to Home Rule in Ulster became powerful and well organised.

4 The threat of armed resistance in Ulster, 1912–14

SOURCE 1

Belfast, under Home Rule – an anti-Home Rule propaganda postcard imagining what Belfast City Hall would come to look like if the southern Irish Catholics were allowed to run the government.

In 1910, in Britain, the Liberals had been re-elected to government, but they needed the support of John Redmond's Irish Parliamentary Party to get their reforms passed. In return Redmond wanted them to introduce a Third Home Rule Bill, which they did in 1912. It failed in the House of Lords again, but the Liberals had passed a law that ruled that the Lords could only delay a bill by two years, not stop it altogether.

In the two years' delay, however, the Unionists took action to stop Home Rule. As a first step, in 1912, half a million Protestant men and women (virtually every Protestant adult in Ulster) signed the 'Solemn League and Covenant', promising to defend 'our cherished position of equal citizenship in the United Kingdom using all means necessary'.

SOURCE 2

On Ulster Day, 28 September 1912, Sir Edward Carson and a huge crowd of Ulster Unionists gathered to sign the Covenant.

Unionist determination to resist Home Rule

In January 1913, the Ulster Volunteer Force, an organisation designed to resist Home Rule by force if necessary, was formed. A hundred thousand men soon enrolled and by April 1914 the UVF had smuggled in 25,000 guns and a million rounds of ammunition at Larne harbour. The weapons came from Germany. The fact that the police turned a blind eye to these events and made no attempt to prevent it, added to the tension in Ulster between Nationalists and Unionists. These were important events and they showed how serious the UVF were in their determination to stop the Liberal government from imposing the Third Home Rule Act on Ulster.

The Nationalist reaction to the formation of the UVF was the formation of the Irish Volunteers in November 1913. By 1914 they too were armed after importing illegal arms through Howth near Dublin.

The situation in Ulster got worse for the Liberal government when, in March 1914, British army officers at the Curragh Barracks near Dublin announced that they would refuse to fight if they were sent to fight the Unionists in Ulster.

The government tried to negotiate. On 21–24 July 1914, King George V held a conference at Buckingham Palace to try to persuade the Unionists to accept 'exclusion' – that the four Ulster counties with Protestant majorities would be left out of the Home Rule agreement. Edward Carson demanded that all six Ulster counties be included, and the conference failed.

It looked like civil war would break out but on 4 August 1914 the First World War broke out instead. The government postponed the introduction of Home Rule.

GET ACTIVE 6

a What does Source 1 tell you about the Ulster Unionists' fears if Home Rule was passed?

b What does Source 2 show about the Ulster resistance to Home Rule in 1912?

c Copy and complete the diagram on the right by adding some details under each of the headings. Use the information on pages 70–71 to help you.

5 The growth of armed Nationalism, 1905–1916

In the last years of the nineteenth century and the early years of the twentieth, many Irish people developed their national identity by taking an increasing interest in Irish language, history and culture. The panel below shows you some of the key factors that influenced the growth of extreme Nationalism in these years.

Conradh na Gaeilge *(the Gaelic League) was founded in 1893 by Douglas Hyde, a Protestant from Roscommon. It promoted Gaelic language, culture and sports.*

After 1908, the Irish Republican Brotherhood *was taken over by young men dedicated to winning independence – for example, Patrick Pearse was Director of Organisation on its secret Supreme Council.*

Arm Cathartha na hÉireann *(the Irish Citizen Army) was formed in 1912 after police had attacked striking transport workers. James Connolly became its leader; he believed that only a free Ireland could protect Irish workers.*

Sinn Féin *('We ourselves') was a political party formed in 1905 by Arthur Griffith, a Nationalist printer. It believed that the Act of Union was illegal, and wanted Irish MPs to boycott the English Parliament and declare independence.*

GET ACTIVE 7

a Go back to page 69 and find the information about John Redmond. How do the ideas in Source 1 differ from Redmond's?

b Use the information in the panel on this page to give reasons why some Nationalists would have supported the ideas of *Sinn Féin* instead of Redmond's.

By 1914, most moderate Nationalists still supported John Redmond but there was a growing number of more radical and extreme Nationalists who were plotting rebellion.

The Easter Rising

As the First World War continued, some Irish Nationalists thought 'England's difficulty is Ireland's opportunity' and therefore decided to take matters into their own hands. In spring 1916 they planned an armed uprising against the British government. Frustrated that the movement for independence had been postponed, they organised a rebellion for Easter 1916.

The plan was as follows. On Good Friday, 21 April, a Nationalist called Roger Casement was to land 20,000 guns and ammunition from Germany. This would arm the Volunteers who could then start a rebellion. However, the British Navy intercepted the arms ship and captured Casement.

Nevertheless, on Easter Monday, 24 April 1916, Pearse, Connolly and a group of about a thousand Nationalists seized key points in Dublin, setting up their HQ in the Post Office building. Pearse then read out the Proclamation of Independence.

The British Army was taken by surprise and it took a week of hard fighting to defeat the rebellion. The Nationalists recorded 64 killed. The British Army reported casualties of 116 dead, 368 wounded and nine missing. Only on 29 April was Pearse forced to surrender.

SOURCE 2

We declare the right of the people of Ireland ... to be sovereign ... The long usurpation of that right by a foreign people and government has not extinguished the right ... We hereby proclaim the Irish Republic as a Sovereign Independent State, and we pledge our lives and the lives of our comrades-in-arms to the cause of its freedom.

Pearse's Proclamation of the Republic, 24 April 1916.

GET ACTIVE 8

a List all the ways the Easter Rising was a failure, and all the ways it was a success.

b Look at Source 4. What makes you suspect that the artist had Nationalist sympathies?

c If you had been an adviser in the British government in 1920 what advice would you have given about how to settle the conflict in Ireland?

SOURCE 3

Buildings in Dublin damaged by British shellfire, 1916.

SOURCE 4

A romantic view of the scene inside the Post Office. Notice Connolly, on a stretcher, with Pearse stood by him. What do you notice about the way their faces are painted? (Clue: look at the photographs on page 72.)

The road to independence

The Easter Rising was not popular with the general public in Ireland because of the destruction to Dublin streets and loss of jobs that followed. As they were led away, Pearse and the rebels were pelted with rubbish and rotten fruit.

However, public attitudes were soon changed by the government's actions after the rebellion. Three thousand people were arrested, 90 people were condemned to death, and 15 of the leaders were actually executed. These executions shocked many people and made the British government very unpopular in Ireland. The government's actions had turned the rebels into martyrs and membership of *Sinn Féin* began to soar.

In 1918, there was a general election in Ireland. Just before it, the government announced that it intended to CONSCRIPT Irish men into the army for the war. The timing could not have been worse. *Sinn Féin* won 73 of the 105 seats. The *Sinn Féin* MPs refused to take their seats at the English Parliament, and instead set up their own parliament – the *Dáil Éireann* – in Dublin and declared independence.

The Irish Volunteers renamed themselves the Irish Republican Army. Led by Michael Collins, they soon clashed with the police and the British Army during the War of Independence, 1919–1921. Atrocities were committed on both sides – for example, on 21 November 1920 a specialist IRA unit called 'the Squad' killed 14 people suspected of being spies for the British. A few hours later the Black and Tans killed 12 people and wounded 60 others in Croke Park, Dublin, during a Gaelic football match. This day was known as Bloody Sunday.

Both sides suffered in the war, and a truce was signed on 11 July 1921.

GET ACTIVE 9

Copy and complete the concept map below. Add details in each circle to show the reasons for the rise of *Sinn Féin*. Compare your points with a partner and discuss any differences.

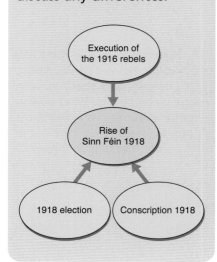

Execution of the 1916 rebels

Rise of Sinn Féin 1918

1918 election

Conscription 1918

People flee as the Black and Tans conduct a raid in Dublin, 1921.

WHY DID LLOYD GEORGE PARTITION IRELAND?

The British Prime Minister, David Lloyd George, was now faced with the task of finding an acceptable solution to the situation in Ireland.

Lloyd George had some sympathy for Home Rule but he did not support independence and had sent the Black and Tans to crush the IRA. At the same time, he knew he could not force Home Rule on the Unionists. On the other hand, he knew that *Sinn Féin* wanted complete independence from Britain. He also realised that he could not defeat the IRA in a war. Moreover, Lloyd George had other problems to deal with as well as settle Ireland, such as the post-war situation in Britain and Europe.

In 1920, while still fighting the IRA, Lloyd George introduced the Government of Ireland Act, which partitioned Ireland. The Act proposed that a six-county state called Northern Ireland be set up with its own parliament in Belfast. A 26-county state called the Free State would rule itself with its own parliament in Dublin, but Britain would still control the army and navy.

This act became law in December 1920 and the *Dáil* agreed on 6 December 1921. Lloyd George had found a compromise that ended the violence in Ireland and saved lives. But while partition may have ended violence in the short term, it stored up problems for the future and laid the seeds of future conflict in Northern Ireland, which we will look at in Chapter 6.

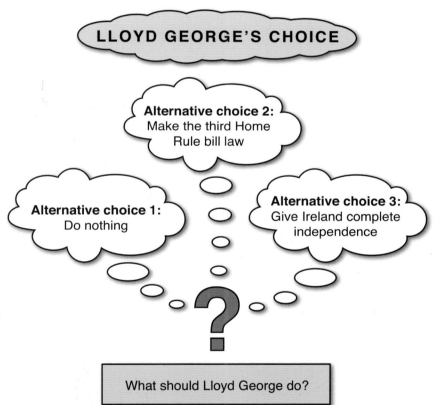

LLOYD GEORGE'S CHOICE

Alternative choice 2: Make the third Home Rule bill law

Alternative choice 1: Do nothing

Alternative choice 3: Give Ireland complete independence

?

What should Lloyd George do?

GET ACTIVE 10

a Copy the diagram above. Take each of the alternatives in turn and make a list of the pros and cons for each one. You may wish to put a plus or minus sign for each of the positive and negative points.

b Explain why you think Lloyd George chose partition as the best solution to the situation in Ireland in 1921.

Plan, Do, Review

You have been investigating the causes of the partition of Ireland. Your task now will be to write your own explanation about the causes of partition. You will carry out this task in three stages and in the final stage you will use a writing frame to help you organise your ideas.

PLAN

This chapter has suggested that there were FIVE underlying causes of partition.

Work with a partner and look at these causes. Go back through the chapter together and make sure you know what each of the causes in the diagram below means:

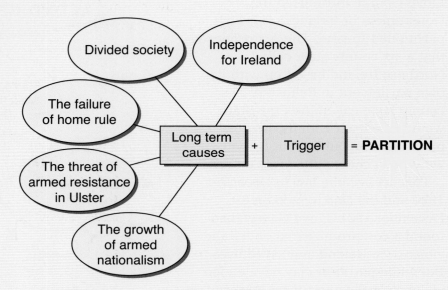

Analyse the causes – can you identify examples of political, economic, cultural and religious factors for causing division?

DO

Stage 1

● In pairs, take each one of the causes and explain HOW it caused partition. The first one is done for you:

> Cause 1 – Independence for Ireland
> This helped to cause partition because it divided Ireland politically into those people who wanted to end British rule in Ireland and those people who wanted to keep British rule in Ireland.

Now do the same for the other four causes.

● Organise the five causes in order of importance. Discuss your ideas with other people in the class. What do you notice about the choices different people have made? Are they similar or different to your choices? Now make a final judgement on the order in which you think the causes should go, depending on which played the biggest part in making partition happen in 1921.

> Long-term Cause 1
> • One of the reasons Ireland was partitioned in 1921 was ...
> • ... [Give some facts]
> • This helped caused partition to happen because ...

Stage 2

● A 'trigger' event is one that happens immediately before a big event. Tensions may have been growing for a long time, but the 'trigger' is the event that 'sets the ball rolling'.

> 'Trigger'
> • The 'trigger' event that led to partition in 1921 was ...
> • [Give some facts]
> • This triggered partition because ...

● Look back at pages 73–74 Can you suggest any events that could be described as a trigger? Again, discuss your ideas with other people in the class to make a final decision.

> Conclusion
> • The most important cause of partition in 1921 was ...
> • I think this because ...

REVIEW

1 Answer the questions below with the responses 'extremely', 'very', 'somewhat' or 'not at all'.
  ● How important is it for Irish student to learn this topic?
  ● How interesting have you found this topic?
  ● How useful did you find the writing frame when writing your essay?
2 Finally, discuss your answers in a small group.

6 What were the consequences of partition for Northern Ireland?

In this chapter we are learning to:
- ✓ explore and link complex historical events and changes;
- ✓ understand how the Troubles started in Northern Ireland;
- ✓ appreciate that the consequences of partition still affect Northern Ireland today;
- ✓ use a visual representation to demonstrate your learning.

A DIVIDED IRELAND

As you work your way through this chapter you will understand the effects or consequences that partition had on Ireland and how some of these still affect our lives today.

The images on this page point to a number of tangible results of partition. As you study the rest of this chapter, you will come to realise that partition also had a significant and lasting effect on the lives of the people who lived there.

GET ACTIVE 1

a With a partner, look at all the pictures on this page. Write down FOUR practical results of partition that you can see. Which of them still apply today?

b Can you think of any other changes you would notice when travelling south of the border? (Think about: what happens to your mobile phone/money/language.)

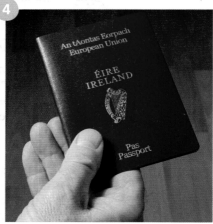

Terms of the Anglo-Irish Treaty

Ireland:

- was to be called the 'Irish Free State';
- would rule itself and have its own parliament;
- was still part of the British Empire;
- had to allow the British control of three ports in Ireland;
- had to make its own MPs take an oath of allegiance to the crown;
- had to allow Northern Ireland to opt out of the Free State.

GET ACTIVE 2

a With a partner, read the terms of the Anglo-Irish Treaty. One of you should choose words from the list below that a supporter of the Treaty might use to describe how they felt about the Treaty. The other should choose words that an opponent of the Treaty might use. Compare your answers and explain your choices to each other.

disappointed, betrayed, hopeful, fearful, angry, frustrated, determined, realistic, threatened, abandoned

b Look at the timeline below, which gives you an overview of the key events in both states in Ireland after partition. Compare and contrast events in both north and south up to 1998. What similarities and differences do you notice?

In the south ...		In the north ...
	1921	Sectarian violence in Northern Ireland.
Civil War in Ireland. **1922–23**	**1922**	The Unionists established control over the government.
Ireland adopted a new CONSTITUTION that claimed Northern Ireland. **1937**		
There was a new IRA campaign of violence against Britain. **1939**		
The Free State government remained neutral during the Second World War. **1939–45**	**1939–45**	Northern Ireland enters the Second World War as part of the United Kingdom.
Britain offered to end partition in return for support in the Second World War. **1940**		
The Republic of Ireland was created. **1949**	**1944–48**	The Welfare State was introduced into Northern Ireland.
	1950s	An IRA campaign against partition failed to get support from the Catholics in the north.
	1960s	A 30-year period of violence called 'the Troubles' broke out in Ulster.
	1970s	Northern Ireland came under direct rule from Westminster (until 1998).
The Republic moved gradually towards more cooperation with the Unionist government in the north. **1960–90**	**1980s**	A number of attempts at power sharing and moves towards peace in Northern Ireland failed.

The jointly-agreed GOOD FRIDAY AGREEMENT: **1998**

- set up a power-sharing Northern Ireland Assembly (which ended direct rule);
- set up a North–South Ministerial Council to bring about cross-border cooperation;
- recognised the British–Irish Inter-governmental Conference;
- set up a British–Irish Council to discuss matters such as health, tourism and transport;
- abolished the Republic of Ireland's historical territorial claim to Northern Ireland;
- recognised the right of all the people of Northern Ireland to identify themselves and be accepted as Irish or British, or both, as they chose.

SOURCE 1

If the Treaty were accepted, the fight for freedom would still go on, and the Irish people, instead of fighting foreign soldiers, will have to fight the Irish soldiers of an Irish government set up by Irishmen.

Speech by Eamon De Valera, leader of the Anti-Treaty IRA, in March 1922.

SOURCE 2

Michael Collins, leader of the Free State forces 1922–23

IMMEDIATE CONSEQUENCES OF PARTITION

Civil War in the Free State

After Ireland was partitioned in 1921, a Civil War was fought in the Free State between January 1922 and May 1923. On the one side was the Free State army, set up by the Anglo-Irish Treaty, and on the other side was the anti-Treaty Republican forces made up of many IRA men. The first few months of the war saw the IRA raiding police barracks for arms and ammunition, and fighting taking place in many towns. When the pro-Treaty *Sinn Féin* won the 1922 election in June the violence increased and the fighting became an all-out GUERILLA WAR between the two sides, which lasted for eight months.

Sectarian violence in the North

In the north the situation was very different to that in the south. By the 1921 Treaty, Northern Ireland had chosen to remain in the United Kingdom. In May 1921 Ulster held its first elections. The Unionists won 40 out of the 52 seats and James Craig became Prime Minister. In June 1921, King George V opened the first Northern Ireland parliament in the City Hall in Belfast.

The new Unionist government found itself under fierce attack from the IRA, and it took measures to safeguard the state by passing the Special Powers Act, giving the police power to arrest suspects without trial ('INTERNMENT').

The years 1920–1922 were very violent. The IRA killed Protestant farmers, mainly in border areas, and reports of Protestants in the south being forced from their homes added to the tension between the two communities in Northern Ireland. This led to sectarian riots, during which around 500 people (Catholics, Protestants and police) were killed, thousands of Catholics lost their jobs and many Catholic houses and businesses were destroyed.

SOURCE 3

The photo shows a train blown up by the IRA near Newry County Down in 1921. IRA violence was to carry on in Northern Ireland throughout the 1920s.

B-SPECIALS in 1920, who were a mainly Protestant Special Constabulary set up to help restore order.

GET ACTIVE 3

a Make a list of the ways in which fighting over the Treaty was different in the south and north.

b What actions did the Unionist government take to safeguard the state in the 1920s?

c What does Source 3 tell you about the attitude of the IRA to partition? How do you think the Unionist government would respond if IRA violence continued after 1921?

SOURCE 1

James Craig was the first Prime Minister of Northern Ireland from 1921–1940. He helped to organise Unionist opposition to Home Rule before 1914 and became leader of the Unionist party in 1921. He made the statement below in April 1934 in response to the claim made by De Valera, the south's leader, that Ireland was a Catholic nation.

'I am an Orangeman first and a politician and member of this parliament afterwards. All I boast is that we are a Protestant parliament and Protestant state.'

EVENTS IN NORTHERN IRELAND 1920–1960s

In this section you will look at events from the perspective of a Unionist and a Nationalist and use sources to find out why both sides came to fear and distrust each other.

Not all people in Northern Ireland supported the Unionist government. One in three of the population in the north were Catholics and they were now a minority in Northern Ireland. They felt isolated from the rest of the Nationalist population in the Free State and they felt that the Unionists wanted to exclude them from government. The Unionist government had 40 seats in the new government and the Nationalists held 12 seats. Between 1922 and 1924 the government had gained control of the local councils by having election boundaries redrawn. This system of election fixing was called gerrymandering and under this system the Unionists were able to get a Unionist council elected even though in some cases, like Londonderry, the Nationalists had a majority. In protest, Nationalist MPs refused to take their seats and withdrew from the government until 1926.

SOURCE 2

Gerrymandering was the term used to describe the fixing of the electoral boundaries so that city councils were controlled by Unionists. This diagram shows an example of gerrymandering in the city of Londonderry where the majority of voters were Catholics but were squeezed into one voting area called the South Ward. The 9,000 Protestant voters were represented by 12 Unionist councillors in the other two wards. The 14,000 Catholics voters were represented by only eight Nationalist councillors.

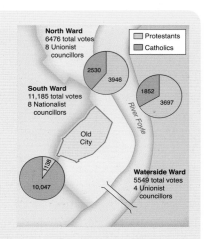

Further divisions were to be seen in the education system, which meant Catholics and Protestants went to separate schools. They also attended separate churches and had separate workplaces.

During the 1930s, both communities suffered great hardship as unemployment reached high levels due to the effects of the Great Depression. Northern Ireland suffered the worst poverty of the UK during these years and by 1932 both Catholic and Protestant workers protested for better wages and improved working conditions.

SOURCE 3

1937	De Valera introduced a new constitution for the Free State (Eire). It claimed the right to rule Northern Ireland, said that a President and not the King of England would be head of the Irish state, and guaranteed a special place in the constitution for the Catholic Church.
1939	The Irish Free State remained neutral during the war with Hitler, and the IRA even started a new campaign of violence in England.
1941	The Free State sent fire engines across the border to help deal with the destruction caused by the Belfast Blitz.
1946	The introduction of the Welfare State to Northern Ireland provided a system of care and benefits which was not available south of the border.
1949	Eire declared itself a 26-county Republic of Ireland.
1956–62	An IRA campaign fizzled out due to lack of support.

In 1937 Eamon De Valera became leader of the Free State. He introduced a new constitution for the Free State, or Eire, as it was to be known.

When the Second World War broke out in 1939, Northern Ireland as part of the UK played a full part and 40,000 men from Northern Ireland fought in the British army against Germany. The Harland and Wolff shipyard contributed over 3,000 ships to the war effort. In 1941, during the Belfast Blitz, German aircraft bombed Belfast in a series of raids which killed over 700 people. After the war, between 1945 and 1950, the British government set up the Welfare State. This introduced free secondary education and a free National Health service. The Welfare State was extended to Northern Ireland and brought about great changes in healthcare, social services and education. Moreover, in 1947, a Housing Trust was set up to build 100,000 new houses.

By 1950 unemployment benefit and pension schemes were in place. These reforms brought prosperity to Northern Ireland and both communities enjoyed their benefits.

In 1956 the IRA began a new campaign of violence and attacked police and military targets along the border, and for a time internment without trial was introduced. The improvements in people's prosperity in the north, which the Welfare State had helped to bring about, had a big impact on this IRA campaign and by 1962 they had to abandon their campaign due to lack of support.

GET ACTIVE 4

You are going to work in pairs to complete two 'living graphs' for people in Northern Ireland between the 1920s and 1960s.

a First look back over the information on pages 80–83 and create a list of events. You may want to sort the events into big themes, such as bad relations/divisions/economy/government, etc.

b Now look at the events from the perspective of most Unionists living in Ulster, marking on the graph for each event whether they would be happy or unhappy about the development. Connect the points to make a 'living graph'.

c Repeat this, looking at events from a mainly Nationalist point of view.

d Finally, use all the information on pages 80–83 to write a paragraph explaining HOW partition caused tension in Northern Ireland between the two communities.

ONE STATE BUT A DIVIDED PEOPLE

In this section we will look at the divisions between Nationalists and Unionists in Northern Irish society.

By the 1960s the number of secondary schools had doubled but the education system was still very SEGREGATED, and while Protestants and Catholics had opportunities to meet at universities and colleges, most school children played different sports and rarely met each other socially. Many workplaces were also segregated and if you happened to live in a mainly Protestant or Catholic populated town or village, it was possible to go to work, live with and speak with only members of your own community.

By the mid-60s many Catholics began to make claims of discrimination against the Unionist government, especially in terms of allocation of houses and jobs. Catholics rarely got top civil service or government jobs. Council houses were not given out fairly, especially to Catholics.

While there had been a rise in the standards of living for people in the late 1950s and early 1960s, the economy was facing serious problems. In 1966 the rope works factory in Belfast closed and at the same time Harland and Wolff, which was the biggest employer in Northern Ireland, closed a number of its shipyards. These closures caused a big rise in unemployment as both industries employed large numbers of people. These economic problems affected both Catholics and Protestants as figures for this period show that Northern Ireland had the highest unemployment rate in all of the UK.

By the late 1960s, the protests over housing focused mainly on Catholics but many Protestant families lived in overcrowded and very poor housing conditions too. Despite the improvements in the number of new houses built under the Welfare State in 1945, Northern Ireland had some of the worst slum housing in Europe at this time.

GET ACTIVE 5

Use the sources and information on pages 82–83.

a Make a list of the ways in which the two communities in Northern Ireland were divided.

b Look at Sources 2 and 4. How do they agree with and differ from each other?

c Look at Sources 1 and 3. What do they show about the living conditions of some Catholics and Protestants?

d A bio poem is a short poem with information about who a person is and how they feel about certain things.

Create two bio-poems about the effects that partition has on i) a Nationalist and ii) a Unionist. Use the sentence stems below to help you

- My name is ...
- I live in ...
- I feel that ...
- I need ...
- I want ...
- I believe ...
- I don't speak to ...
- I would like to see ...
- I distrust ...
- My feelings about partition are ...

Harland and Wolff was the biggest employer in Northern Ireland up to 1966 when it closed down many of its shipyards.

Slum housing conditions in the mainly Protestant area of Belfast in the 1960s.

Extract from No Surrender *by R. Harbinson, a Protestant describing growing up in a Protestant area.*

Our schools drummed into us over and over again the Protestant story. Our ignorance of the Catholic world was profound. I for instance believed that Catholics existed only in parts of Belfast and nowhere else but the Free State and Rome itself.

Slum housing conditions in the mainly Catholic Londonderry in the 1960s.

An extract from a book called the Price of My Soul *by Bernadette Devlin (who was a leading figure in radical student group called the* PEOPLE'S DEMOCRACY*) describing her education at Catholic Grammar School in the 1960s.*

We learned Irish history. We were all learning the same things, the same events, the same period of time, but the interpretations were different.

WHY WAS THERE A CIVIL RIGHTS MOVEMENT IN 1967?

Inspired by these new traditions of peaceful protest against civil injustices in America, a group of people formed a Northern Ireland Civil Rights Association (NICRA) in February 1967. This group was made up of both Catholic and Protestant students, some middle-class Protestants, and many Catholics who wanted to draw attention to the need for social reform in Northern Ireland. (You will learn more about the methods of the NICRA on page 88.)

The introduction of the Welfare State in the 1940s had made secondary education free for everyone and this resulted in a new younger generation of well-educated Catholics who were now interested in participating in political life in Northern Ireland. They did not want to end partition or to bring down the state of Northern Ireland. Instead they wanted to work to reform the government and abolish discrimination. Many Protestants who had been formerly unaware of discrimination supported the movement.

In the late 1960s across Europe there was a growing interest, especially among students, in political issues such as the Vietnam War. There were many peaceful mass demonstrations on the streets as a way of protesting against government policy. The student members of the NICRA tried to hold their own protests in Northern Ireland but the Unionist government stopped their attempts.

SOURCE 1

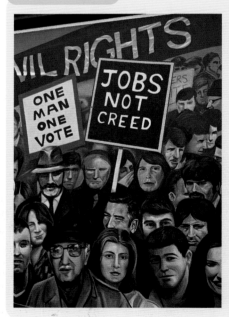

A Civil Rights wall mural from Rossville Street in the Bogside area of Derry, made in 2004, showing the artist's impression of an early Civil Rights march. The placards on the mural show many of the demands of the Civil Rights campaign.

GET ACTIVE 6

a Why was a Civil Rights movement formed in Northern Ireland in 1967?

b Use Source 1. If you were a member of the Unionist government in 1968, how do you think you would react to the formation of the NICRA?

THE OUTBREAK OF THE TROUBLES IN NORTHERN IRELAND

You have looked at events and changes in Northern Ireland in the 40 years after partition. Now we will consider how many of these events led to the outbreak of the Troubles in 1969. Sources 2 to 7 on pages 87–9 record the main stages in the return of violence to Northern Ireland.

SOURCE 2

O'Neill fails to bring reform

In 1963, Terence O'Neill became Prime Minister of Northern Ireland. He seemed less hostile towards Catholics than previous Unionist leaders, and he promised reforms. He wanted to introduce reforms that would modernise the state and create more jobs and industry. He was on friendly terms with the TAOISEACH Sean Lemass but in the end, however, O'Neill's reforms changed very little. Catholics' hopes were disappointed as they had hoped that his government would put an end to discrimination.

GET ACTIVE 7

Look at Sources 2 to 7 on pages 87–9.
a Make a timeline of events 1963–1969.
b Below is a list of triggers that helped cause the outbreak of violence in Northern Ireland in 1969. Take each one and then explain how it may have caused the outbreak of violence:
  • Civil Rights marches
  • O'Neill's reforms
  • The arrival of the British Army
  • The revival of the IRA
c Rank the statements from part b of the activity in order of priority with the trigger you think the most important at the top to the trigger you think least important at the bottom and justify your choices. You could use a priority pyramid to help you with this task.

SOURCE 3

Protestant backlash

O'Neill's reforms were too much for Protestants such as Ian Paisley, who accused O'Neill of being 'soft on Rome'. The UVF reorganised in 1966, and one of their members, 'Gusty' Spence, was imprisoned for the murder of a Catholic. Paisley built strong support among LOYALISTS and Unionists who were opposed to O'Neill's reforms.

SOURCE 4

Civil Rights protest, 1969

Copying the methods of Martin Luther King's American Civil Rights movement in America, the Northern Ireland Civil Rights Association (NICRA) demanded Civil Rights for Catholics and an end to discrimination in jobs and housing.

SOURCE 5

Civil Rights marches, 1969

The NICRA began to organise marches to get publicity for their demands. A march through Londonderry was attacked by police, and the People's Democracy March from Belfast to Derry on 1–4 January (above) was attacked by Protestants and off-duty B-Specials at Burntollet Bridge.

SOURCE 6

Rioting

Unionists and police believed that members of the IRA were involved in the Civil Rights marches. Here, police charge rioting youths, August 1969. Attacks like this led to serious rioting, mainly in Belfast and Derry.

SOURCE 7

The British Army

In August 1969, the British government sent in the army. At first the soldiers were welcomed by the Catholic community, but their raids, curfews and arrests in Catholic areas soon led many Catholics to turn against them. Behind the scenes the PIRA and the old Official IRA were reforming. When the Prime Minister Chicester Clarke ordered the police to search Catholic areas for IRA suspects and arms, the IRA retaliated by attacking Protestant businesses and attacking the British Army and the RUC. The Troubles had begun and were to last for the next 30 years.

MOVING TOWARDS PEACE

In this chapter you have seen how Ireland's history (and Northern Ireland's history) in the twentieth century has been about divisions – the division between north and south, the division between Protestant and Catholic, Unionist and Nationalist, and the division between Britain and Ireland. Between 1969 and 2001 there were over 3,526 people killed in the violence in Northern Ireland, known as the Troubles. Many families are still suffering from these losses today. While the Good Friday Agreement in 1998 ended the 30-year cycle of violence and gave the country its own power-sharing assembly, Ireland is still divided. The grid below lists some of the main events of the Troubles.

1969 to 1994	Paramilitary groups on both sides committed atrocities both in Ulster and on the mainland.	1971	Internment without trial was introduced. The number of terrorist incidents rose markedly.
1972	'Bloody Sunday' – 13 people on a NICRA march died after being shot by British troops in Derry.	1972	Most violent year of the Troubles – 497 people were killed.
1974	A strike – organised by the Loyalist Ulster Workers' Council – caused the collapse of the power-sharing executive.	1976	Women's Peace Movement (later Peace People) was formed and this gained a lot of support from all sides.
1981	IRA prisoners went on hunger strike.	1985	The Anglo–Irish Agreement gave the government of the Republic a say in Northern Ireland's affairs.
1994	PIRA and Loyalist paramilitaries announced ceasefires.	1995	US President Clinton supports the peace talks by visiting Northern Ireland.
1996	Peace talks were chaired by Senator George Mitchell.	1998	Good Friday Agreement.

GET ACTIVE 8

a Study the events in the table above. Identify those that increased the divisions between the different communities. Identify the events that brought the different parties together.

b Apart from the Good Friday Agreement, which other event do you think was most important in bringing the different parties together?

Plan, Do, Review

You have studied a long period of history involving events in both the new states that partition set up. You have seen – because Ireland had been a divided society for many years – how difficult it was and how long it took to get all sides to come to an agreement.

Your task will be to add short- and long-term consequences of partition on the consequence wheel below and then to make any links between them.

PLAN

Gather your ideas.
- Skim through the chapter and make some quick notes on:
  - the short-term consequences
  - the long-term consequences
  - the impact of partition today.

Do you need to do any more research on any key points?

DO

Make a copy of the consequence wheel opposite on a large piece of paper. In your wheel write in short-term and long term consequences of partition, and the impact of partition roday. One example has been done for you. See if you can make links between them and draw lines on your diagram to show the links. Then explain to a partner how they are limited.

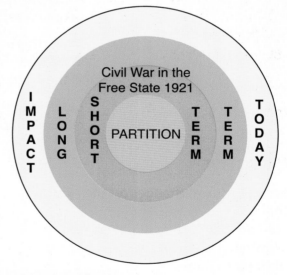

Consequence wheel

REVIEW

1 How successful was using the diagram to help you to organise your ideas?
2 How successful was the consequence wheel in helping you to make links?
3 Can you think of any other form of visual representation you could use to show what you have learned in this chapter?

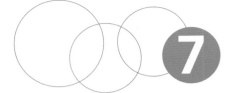

7 Did life get better for ordinary people in the twentieth century?

In this chapter we are learning to:
- ✓ manage information by sorting, classifying and evaluating information;
- ✓ understand the concepts of progression and regression;
- ✓ work together to reach a consensus.

Throughout this book you have been learning about some of the famous people and events of the twentieth century.

In this chapter you are going to examine the century from a different point of view – that of ordinary people who lived here in Northern Ireland or in other parts of the world.

The question you will try to answer is: 'Did life get better for ordinary people in the twentieth century?' That is, was it a century of progress? You will use the knowledge and the skills you have developed throughout our study of the twentieth century to help you in your investigation.

On pages 92–5 you will examine if and how life changed for people locally in:

- Northern Ireland;
- Ireland;
- the United Kingdom.

Later in the chapter you will examine information about changes and developments from around the world.

GET ACTIVE 1

Look at the local changes on the cards on pages 94–5.

a You are going to begin by sorting or classifying the local changes into six different themes:
- communication;
- education;
- health;
- work;
- travel;
- leisure.

i Divide into six groups with each group taking responsibility for one of the themes.

ii Individually, take five minutes to choose which change card matches the group theme.

iii Start sharing your ideas with your group.

iv Discuss each change card until a consensus is reached.

v Copy and complete the first two columns of the table below.

vi Choose two group members to explain your choices to the rest of the class.

Description of change card	What it says about our theme	Links with other themes
Card number:	It shows that . . .	

b Review:

i Many of the changes are INTERDEPENDENT. As you listen to the selection from the other groups complete the third column in the table – links to other themes – and answer the following questions:

• Did you find that some changes fell into more than one theme or category?

• Did some themes have more changes than others?

• Were there some change cards that didn't fall easily into any theme?

ii Make a concept map to show the links between the themes.

GET ACTIVE 2

Your second group task is to decide whether the cards you have selected show that things got better or worse during the last century for ordinary people in Northern Ireland. Are these changes evidence of PROGRESSION or REGRESSION?

a Draw a clothes line across a flip chart page and write 'progress' down the left pole holding up the line and 'regress' down the right pole, as illustrated on the right.

Place each change card on the clothes line according to where your group thinks it belongs. If, for example, you have been selecting the health cards, your group may agree that the discovery of antibiotics was definite progress and place that card closer to the progress pole.

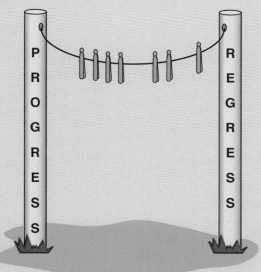

b Review:

i Compare your clothes line with the other groups'. Take it in turns to explain your choices to the rest of the class. Copy and complete the individual summary sheet below as you listen to each group. Keep a tally as each group reports back.

ii Use your tally chart to help you answer the question 'Did life get better for ordinary people in the twentieth century?'

Category	Progression +	Not sure?	Regression –
Transport			
Leisure			
Health			
Communication			
Work			
Education			

LOCAL CHANGES IN THE TWENTIETH CENTURY

A Before the development of cheap airlines, flying was expensive and only very rich people could afford to travel abroad. By 1971, British holidaymakers were taking seven million holidays abroad; by 1987 this figure had risen to 20 million.

B At the beginning of the century people got their information about world events from newspapers. As the century progressed, other forms of media such as radio and, later, television developed. By the end of the century war could even be watched live on television.

C At the beginning of the century secondary education was not free to all. The 1944 Education Act provided free secondary education for everyone until the age of 15. This act was one in a series of steps that gave children chances their parents never had.

D The types of jobs open to women changed over the century. Margaret Thatcher was the first woman Prime Minister of Britain from 1979 to 1990.

E At the beginning of the century, traditional teaching was centred on the three Rs: reading, writing and arithmetic. By the end of the century pupils studied a broader curriculum.

F At the beginning of the century, planned leisure activities were largely confined to the upper classes and mainly involved country pursuits. By the end of the century more people than ever before were participating in planned leisure activities such as going to gyms and fitness clubs.

G At the beginning of the century the most common form of communication was by letter or, in special circumstances, by telegram. By the end of the century the most common form of communication was the mobile phone.

H At the beginning of the century people depended on gas and coal as their main sources of energy. By the end of the century the demand for oil had overtaken these other fossil fuels due to increased dependence on oil for petrol and plastics manufacture.

I At the beginning of the century infectious diseases, such as tuberculosis and cholera, led to many deaths. By the end of the century the discovery and mass production of antibiotics had revolutionised the treatment of disease and infection.

J Towards the second half of the twentieth century bacteria such as MRSA, which was first identified in 1961 in the UK, had become increasingly resistant to antibiotics and therefore far more difficult to treat.

K New technology in hospitals such as MRI scans and kidney dialysis machines advanced throughout the century. This was different from the beginning of the century when technological equipment in hospitals was very limited.

L In the 1970s the personal computer was born and was developed, steadily growing in popularity during the rest of the century. By the end of the century it was used for education, work and leisure.

M Many people at the beginning of the century depended on traditional industries such as shipbuilding for employment. However, this declined over the century. For example, the last liner built at Harland and Wolff was the *Canberra* in 1960 and, by 1989, the number of people employed by the company had fallen to around 3,000.

As manufacturing dwindled in significance, the service sector grew in the Northern Irish economy and by the end of the century it accounted for about three-quarters of jobs.

N Tony Blair stated in his speech to the National Association of Head Teachers in 1999:

'One in five adults [are] functionally illiterate – meaning, in real life, seven million adults [are] unable to find the page reference for plumbers in the Yellow Pages. An even higher proportion, four in ten, are unable to manage basic arithmetic.'

O Working conditions improved during the twentieth century as Trade Unions became more organised. The National Insurance Act of 1911 paved the way for better treatment of workers as it introduced a general fund for sick pay, maternity pay and a measure of unemployment benefits. Later laws would prohibit child labour and set minimum wage levels for workers.

P The 'Enterprise Express' train was introduced on 11 August, 1947, and provided a fast and easy way to get from Belfast to Dublin.

However, the local network of trains in Northern Ireland declined over the century.

Q Travel in 1900 was largely by horse-drawn carriage. The twentieth century saw increasing dependence on the motor car. Figures show that motorists drove 237.75 billion miles in 2000 – the equivalent to travelling to Pluto and back 33 times, and 15 times more than the number of car journeys made in 1950.

R Obesity had become a late twentieth century phenomenon. Surveys carried out in Northern Ireland in the 1990s indicated that in general the number of obese people was increasing. Levels of obesity in children were also increasing. In all, 56 per cent of all those whose height and weight were measured in the 1997 Health and Social Well Being Survey were either overweight (37 per cent) or obese.

S A programme to vaccinate everyone under the age of 15 against polio and diphtheria was launched in 1958.

This programme saw everyone under the age of 15 vaccinated and led to an immediate and dramatic reduction in cases of both diseases.

T The National Health Service was launched in 1948 with the promise to care for the British people from 'the cradle to the grave'. Before this, medical treatment had to be paid for and was very expensive.

Public health and living conditions improved, and new council housing was built after the Second World War.

U In the 1900s the idea of a teenager did not exist as expectations of children were different and they were expected to be 'seen and not heard'. Teenage culture developed over the century as young people began to listen to their own music and dress in their own way. Teenage magazines grew in popularity and these focused on looks, music and love.

CHANGE AND PROGRESS AT A GLOBAL LEVEL

In the previous section your group looked at whether life got better or worse for people living in the UK and Ireland in the last century. In this section you will explore whether this was the same for people living in other parts of the world.

Questions in history, as you have already discovered, are very rarely simple. We are going to complicate the investigation by adding another question: 'If life got better – did it get better for everyone or just a few people?'

The change cards on page 98 have been categorised into: 1) Global Warming, 2) Education, 3) Global Economy, 4) Cultural Diversity, 5) Rise of China, 6) Global Health, 7) Child Labour and 8) Nuclear Threat.

GET ACTIVE 3

a Look at each of the issues identified on page 98 and decide whether the issue meant progress for all, for most people, or for very few people. Copy and complete the table below by writing the card number in the most appropriate column. You may find that you can't decide where to place the issue because you require more information. For example, if you were looking at Cultural Diversity you may have questions such as:

- What do countries do with the large number of immigrants who want to settle there?
- Do the governments of these countries send the people back to their country of origin?

The answers to these questions require further information and you may decide to search the UNHCR site (www.unhcr.org.uk) to find out about refugees and asylum seekers before you make your decision.

Impact of issues worldwide			
Need more information	Progress for all	Progress for most people	Progress for very few people

b Appoint someone to stay at your desk with the group's completed table while the rest of the group divide to go to each of the other groups. The remaining group member must explain to the tourists why the decisions were made. You are now going to use your enquiry skills to find examples of progress and regression under another theme – one very close and relevant to everyone – HOMES. Our homes and the way we lived in them certainly changed dramatically during the twentieth century. Technology changed every room in the house and differing fashions and tastes changed the shape and style of our homes.

GET ACTIVE 4

Working once again in the same groups, decide how you are going to show how homes in Northern Ireland changed in the twentieth century, and whether these changes made things better or worse. Your group should prepare to answer the question: 'What did the twentieth century do for homes? Was there progression or regression?'

a Use the school library, history books and the internet to help you with your enquiry. You could also use the evidence all around you.
  - Think about what you have learnt in technology, geography and science classes and discuss your enquiry with your teachers.
  - Think about members of your family and local community who might be able to provide oral or visual evidence of how homes changed in their lifetimes.
  - Think about the different kinds of homes in your area and what has changed.
  - Use local and national newspapers, magazines and TV programmes about home improvement.

b Present your findings as an estate agent's leaflet describing the changes in your twentieth-century home. However, you must decide on the success criteria that will judge your final piece of work. An example of success criteria might be that your piece of work:
  - has a clear heading and introduction;
  - has shown examples of how the home has been improved through the century, for example, location, size, comfort and amenities;
  - contains relevant illustrations or graphics.

1 GLOBAL WARMING

New developments in the century saw an increase in the demand in the developed world for fossil fuels such as oil and coal.

2 EDUCATION

In most countries education changed over the century. For example, in 1970, women made up over 60 per cent of the 10,000 students who studied at Kabul University, Afghanistan, but in 1990, under the Taliban, only about three per cent of girls received some form of primary education. Classroom facilities were not the same everywhere throughout the world. In many developing countries classrooms were overcrowded and under-resourced.

3 GLOBAL ECONOMY

With developments in transport and communications, the global economy expanded and some companies now sell their goods worldwide.

4 CULTURAL DIVERSITY

During the twentieth century over 86 million people moved to a different country to live and work.

5 RISE OF CHINA

China became one of the largest producers of consumer goods in the twentieth century. The use of cheap labour and mass production meant that cheap goods were exported from China to be sold on the global market.

6 GLOBAL HEALTH

HIV/AIDS was first recognised as a disease in December 1981. It has become known as the twentieth century's plague. By 2000, three million people were reported to have died due to AIDS-related illnesses.

The United Nations was set up after the Second World War. It is an international organisation whose aim is to maintain peace and to protect equal human rights across the world. Some of the branches of the UN are the World Health Organisation, UNICEF and UNHCR.

7 CHILD LABOUR

Studies carried out in 1979 found that 50 million children worldwide under the age of 15 were working in various jobs and often in dangerous conditions.

8 NUCLEAR THREAT

In April 1986 one of the four nuclear reactors at Chernobyl power station in Ukraine exploded. The disaster released 100 times more radiation than the atomic bombs at Hiroshima and Nagasaki. It is still not known how many deaths this disaster will cause in total.

Plan, Do, Review

In this chapter you have been looking at how changes in the twentieth century impacted on people locally and globally. You are now going to use your knowledge to create a Progress and Regress snakes and ladders game.

PLAN

Develop the success criteria for this activity and use the suggestions below to help you draw up a 'to do' list for your project. You will need to:

- select changes that show progression. These will be the squares at the bottom of your ladders.
- select changes that are examples of regression. These will be at the top of your snakes.

DO

- Draw out your snakes and ladders board. You could use the computer to help with

this task, creating an 8x8 chequer board like the one below.
- Decide how many snakes and ladders you are going to have.
- Decide where you are going to draw your snakes and ladders on the board.

REVIEW

Take some time to reflect on this activity and write a short diary considering three areas:

- What you have been learning about the twentieth century and your conclusion as to whether things did get better for ordinary people.
- How well did you work as a group? Did everyone take on a role and contribute to the shared tasks? Were you a good group member?
- How would you help your group do better next time?

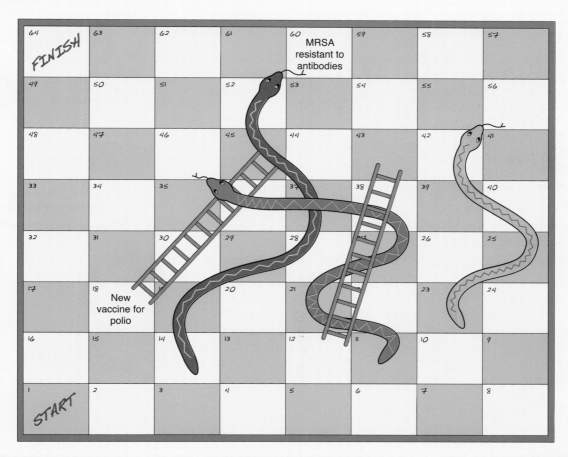

99

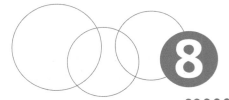

8 Getting better at history

 In this chapter we are learning to:
- ✓ review our learning and the way we have learned throughout the book;
- ✓ set and evaluate performance outcomes against agreed success criteria;
- ✓ select and evaluate information from a range of sources;
- ✓ manage time.

WHAT SPECIALIST TERMINOLOGY HAVE YOU LEARNED IN THIS BOOK?

Throughout the book you have met with many historical terms and words that help historians describe accurately events and changes that happened in the twentieth century.

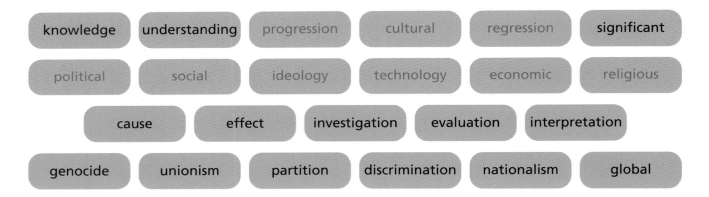

knowledge   understanding   progression   cultural   regression   significant

political   social   ideology   technology   economic   religious

cause   effect   investigation   evaluation   interpretation

genocide   unionism   partition   discrimination   nationalism   global

GET ACTIVE 1

a Look at this example of the definition of the term ideology:
'ideology' means a set of attitudes, beliefs and ideas, usually about politics.

b Now make your own definitions for the remaining eight concepts in pink, representing them visually as an appropriate picture.

c Do you know what all the other words mean, and can you say where you met them in studying this textbook?

Thoughts, ideas and beliefs about politics

WHAT HISTORY SKILLS HAVE YOU DEVELOPED IN THIS BOOK?

As you have been studying the events and developments of the twentieth century, you have learned that you have to use historians' skills to organise and analyse the different information and sources. Get Active 2 will allow you to think about how well you can use these 'historians' skills'.

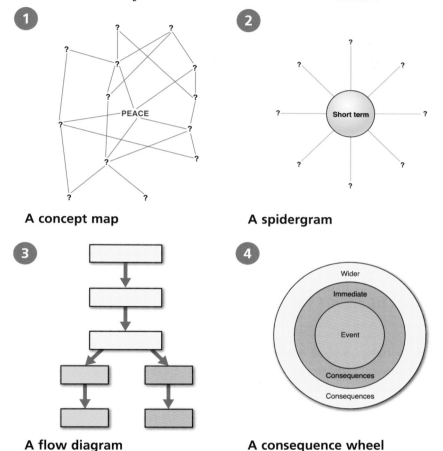

A concept map

A spidergram

A flow diagram

A consequence wheel

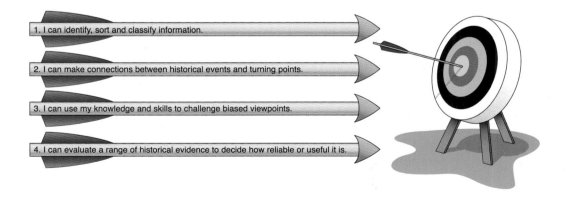

1. I can identify, sort and classify information.

2. I can make connections between historical events and turning points.

3. I can use my knowledge and skills to challenge biased viewpoints.

4. I can evaluate a range of historical evidence to decide how reliable or useful it is.

WHICH FACTOR HAS BEEN MOST IMPORTANT IN THE TWENTIETH CENTURY?

You are now going to use all your historians' skills to make a presentation on the factors that influenced human behaviour in the twentieth century.

Step 1
Here are some factors:

**Political – Social – Economic – Cultural – Ideology
Religious – Technology – War – Health**

Which factor do you think was the most important? Were twentieth-century people more inclined to the 'political' than the religious? Were they more affected by 'social' issues than by 'economic' factors? Were their influences 'ideological' or 'cultural'? Or have the most significant developments been in 'technology'?

Use a 'diamond nine' diagram to help you arrange the list of factors (see left). The most important reason is put at the top of the diagram, and the other reasons you think are important are arranged below. The least important reasons are put at the bottom.

SELECT THE MOST IMPORTANT FACTOR

Step 2
You now have to find evidence to back up your choices in the last question. This textbook will be your first source of information. You may wish to use other sources, such as the internet/your local library/TV documentaries, etc.

Step 3
You must now organise your ideas and information ready to research for your presentation. In the presentation, you will need to:

● give two or more examples of events where your factor influenced people's behaviour;
● give two or more reasons of how those events were historically significant.

Use one of the diagrams on page 99 to help you organise your ideas. Choose the method that will be best to help you explain how each factor affected people's behaviour.
  Set yourself a time deadline, and keep to it.

Having collected all your evidence, create your visual diagram and then share your work with the rest of the class, explaining what it means.

Step 4

Now you are ready to produce your presentation, using the frame below to help you! Using the outline on this page, follow the steps described in the diagram below.

Conclusion

Draw all of your points together. Refer specifically back to the question and conclude with how your key factor is most important. Summarise the reasons you have given and the evidence you have found. Finish with the statement: 'Therefore, we can conclude that the twentieth century was primarily an age of . . .'

Decide on your script and the images and sound you will put with each frame of your presentation.
Remember the rest of your class is your audience and you have to make a reasoned argument to convince them why your factor is the most important.

Section 2:
For each of your events, explain why they were significant.

This was significant because ...

Section 1:
Give two examples of where your factor played a part.

This affected ...

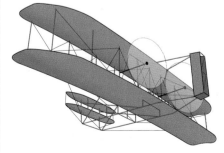

Introduction

Set the scene for the presentation by stating clearly what your factor is and explain why you have chosen it. Perhaps you will outline the type of evidence/sources of information you will use to convince the reader/listener that your factor of change is the most important.

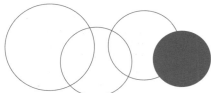

Glossary

Anti-Semitism Racial prejudice or hostility towards Jews

Arms Race Competition between countries to achieve superiority in quantity and quality of military arms

B-Specials A reserve police force also known as the Ulster Special Constabulary, formed in 1920. A mainly Protestant force that came to be mistrusted by Catholics in Northern Ireland

Blockade An attempt to cut off a country's communications by land, air or sea, using force

British Empire The term used to describe the areas of the world under British rule between the late sixteenth century and the mid twentieth century

Censor A government official who has the power to suppress information considered insensitive and damaging to the safety of the country, especially in times of war

Cold War The term used to describe the state of tension and hostility that existed after the Second World War between the Soviet Union and the countries under its control, and the western world led by the United States

Colony A piece of land or territory under the control of another state

Communism A set of political ideas that promotes a classless society. In a Communist society people make the same wages, making everyone equal, and there is no private ownership. Under a Communist government there is only one party to vote for, namely the Communists

Conscript Person who is drafted into the armed services involuntarily

Conscientious objector Someone who refuses on moral or religious grounds to bear arms in a military conflict or to serve in the armed forces

Conservatives The term used to describe a British parliamentary party founded in the early nineteenth century. This party was opposed to Home Rule and it supported the Ulster Unionists in their resistance to Home Rule

Constitution A set of laws by which a country is governed

Court martial A military court that decides punishments according to military law

Democracy Government by the people: a form of government in which the supreme power is vested in the people and exercised directly by them or by their elected agents under a free electoral system

Disarmament The act of laying down arms, especially the reduction or abolition of a nation's military forces and armaments

Discrimination To treat a person or groups of people differently than others

Evacuate Remove persons or things from a dangerous place

Fenians The name given to a group of Irish Republicans whose aim was to create an independent republic for Ireland in the nineteenth century, using physical force if necessary. Today, Fenian is a term used to describe supporters of Irish Nationalism

Final Solution The name given to the mass murder of the Jews in Europe under the Nazis in Germany between 1941 and 1945

First plantations The sixteenth-century system whereby the English government sent over settlers to live and work on confiscated lands of the Gaelic chiefs in Ireland

Führer Leader of the Nazi state

Genocide Violent crimes committed against groups of people so that they don't exist anymore

Glasnost A policy of openness in the activities of the government of the Soviet Union introduced by Mikhail Gorbachev in the 1980s

Good Friday Agreement An agreement between the British and Irish governments to end the Troubles in Northern Ireland and signed

Great Depression
by all the political parties of Northern Ireland in 1998
A worldwide economic crisis that originated in the United States and followed the crash of the American stock exchange on 29 October, 1929. This led to a decade of poverty, unemployment, and low wages in many countries of the world

Guerilla war
Where a small army uses tactics such as ambushes and raids to fight a larger and usually more organised army

Home Rule
A movement in nineteenth-century Ireland for internal self-government, but with Britain controlling Ireland's foreign affairs

Imperialism
The policy of extending the rule or authority of an empire or nation over foreign countries, or of acquiring and holding colonies and dependencies

Interdependent
When two states cooperate with each other they are said to be interdependent

Internment
Imprisonment without trial

Irish Republican Brotherhood
A secret oath-bound movement founded in the USA by John O. Mahoney and pledged to winning independence for Ireland by force

Irish Volunteers
An organisation founded in 1913 to safeguard the passing of Home Rule in Ireland

IRA
Irish Republican Army; a military organisation founded in 1913 and pledged to winning independence for Ireland by ending British rule by force

Liberals
The term used to describe a British Liberal parliamentary party founded in the nineteenth century. It was Liberal Prime Minister Gladstone who introduced the first two Home Rule Bills for Ireland in 1886 and 1893. Today, this party is known as the Liberal Democrats

Loyalists
Originally a term used to describe Protestants who were opposed to Catholic Emancipation and greater independence for Ireland in the nineteenth century. In the twentieth century it came to mean people who were loyal to the British government, the Queen and the Ulster Unionist party

Marshall Aid
Financial aid given to western European countries by the USA to assist their economic recovery after the Second World War. It was part of a plan called the Marshall Plan, named after George Marshall, the US Secretary of State who organised it

Militant
Using violent rather than peaceful means

Nationalist
A supporter of independence for Ireland in the nineteenth century who admired Irish culture, language and history. Today the term can be used to describe someone who might support the reunification of Ireland

Nazi
The National Socialist party formed in Germany in 1919 and led by Adolf Hitler. This party was in power in Germany from 1933 to 1945

No Man's Land
A term used to describe the area of land between two enemy trenches that neither side could take control of for fear of being attacked

Pacifist
A person who is opposed to war or violence as a way of settling a dispute

Papist
A derogatory word used to imply the loyalties of Roman Catholics are with the papacy in Rome.

Partition
The division of a country with a boundary between each part

People's Democracy
The People's Democracy was a radical student group founded in 1968 at Queen's University, Belfast, which aimed to establish a socialist republic for all of Ireland. This group supported the campaign for Civil Rights for Catholics in Northern Ireland and organised the People's Democracy March in 1968 from Belfast to Londonderry in January 1969

Perestroika
The changes in the Soviet economy and administration that took place under Mikhail Gorbachev's rule in the 1980s

Philanthropist
Someone who makes charitable donations intended to increase human well-being

PIRA
Provisional Irish Republican Army: a military organisation, formed in 1969 to drive the British forces from Northern Ireland and obtain the reunification of Ireland

Pogrom
A Russian word meaning violent attacks on Jews

Posthumous	Awarded after death
Prejudice	Feelings and attitudes of hostility towards a group of people or individuals without reason or knowledge
Progression	The advances in people's lives across a period of time
Propaganda	Material disseminated or given out by the advocates or opponents of a doctrine or cause. In wartime, propaganda is used by both sides to raise morale at home and discourage the enemy
Protestant Ascendancy	The name given to a group of landowners and clergy who dominated Irish political and social life from the seventeenth to nineteenth centuries
Regression	How people's lives changed for the worse across a period of time
Sectarianism	Describes a set of narrow religious or political beliefs by members of a group that leads to bigotry, discrimination, and intolerance
Segregation	The separation of different groups of people. Can be based on race, religion or political beliefs
Sinn Féin	A Republican political party founded in 1905 and committed to the establishment of an Irish republic
Soviet Union	*See* USSR
Stereotyping	Preconceived ideas about groups of people, usually based on physical appearance
Suffrage	The right to vote in a political election
Taoiseach	The head of the government in the Republic of Ireland
The Troubles	The term used to describe a period of violence in Northern Ireland that lasted from 1969 to 1998
Ulster Division	The name given to a group of soldiers made up of members of the Ulster Volunteer Force. They were formed into the 36th division in September 1914 and fought for Britain on the Western Front during the First World War, 1914–1918
Unionist	A person who wants Northern Ireland to remain part of the United Kingdom
United Irishmen	A political group founded in the eighteenth century to reform the Irish Parliament and who in 1798 organised a rebellion to end British rule in Ireland in order to establish an independent Irish republic
United Nations	An international organisation founded in 1945 to achieve world peace
USSR	The Union of the Soviet Socialist Republic: formed in 1924 and dissolved in 1991, it was made up of Russia and her allies
UVF	Ulster Volunteer Force: formed in 1913 to resist Home Rule
VC	The Victoria Cross: the highest honour awarded to a soldier in the British army, for exceptional acts of bravery during a war. It was introduced in 1856 under Queen Victoria
Wall Street Crash	The collapse of the stock exchange in America in October 1929. It was the beginning of a chain of events that led to a period of economic decline called the Great Depression
Welfare State	The name given to a series of government reforms introduced in 1945 that set up and financed a system of care and benefits for everyone who needed it, from the cradle to the grave
Workhouse	A place where people who could not support themselves could go to live and work. Workhouses were formed in Ireland in 1838 under the terms of the Irish Poor Law Act and were run by a Board of Guardians who had the power to decide on admissions and discipline inside the workhouse, which at times could be harsh

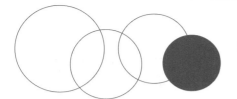

Index

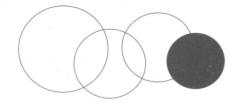

Photo credits and acknowledgements

p14 Dr Tabuchi diary entry, 7 August 1945, from *Hiroshima Diary: The Journal of a Japanese Physician, August 6 – September 30, 1945* by Michihiko Hachiya © University of North Carolina Press, 1955; **p25**, First World War diary of Emma Duffin © Public Records Office of Northern Ireland; **p32** website text and logo © Amnesty International; **p59** lines from 'The Berlin Wall' from *A Tall, Serious Girl* by George Stanley © Qua Books, 2003

p10 *t* © NASA, *bl* © Corbis, *br* © LUIS ALONSO/EFE/Corbis; **p11** Courtesy of Belfast City Council; **p12** *l* © Hulton-Deutsch Collection/Corbis, *r* © A Chederros/Onoky/ Photolibrary.com; **p14** © Bettmann/Corbis; **p18** *l* © Bettmann/Corbis, *r* © Corbis; **p19** *t* © Bettmann/Corbis, *b* © Neal Preston/Corbis; **p22** *t* © Paul Collis/Alamy, *b* Courtesy of Belfast City Council; **p23** © Bettmann/Corbis; **p24** *tl* © Corbis, *tr* © Lordprice Collection/Alamy, *cl* akg-images *cr* © David Spurdens/Corbis, *b* © Sylvia Cordaiy Photo Library Ltd/Alamy; **p25** AP/Press Association Images; **p26** *t* © Corbis, *b* © Camille Moirenc/Hemis/Corbis; **p27** *t* © Bettmann/Corbis, *b* © Vivien Kelly; **p28** *tl* Courtesy Library of Congress/Brown Brothers, *tr* British Pathé Ltd, *bl* © Bettmann/Corbis, *br* © Durand-Hudson-Langevin-Orban/Sygma/Corbis; **p29** © Corbis; **p30** *tl* UN Photo/Paulo Filgueiras, *bl* UN Photo/Gernot Payer, *r* © UNICEF/NYHQ2008-1214/Holt; **p32** *tr* © Mike Goldwater/Alamy, *tl* ©International Federation of Red Cross and Red Crescent Societies, *bl* © David Hoffman/Alamy, *br* Courtesy of Amnesty International UK; **p33** *t* © Bettmann/Corbis, *b* © Topfoto; **p35** *t* © Bettmann/Corbis, *b* © Trinity Mirror/Mirrorpix/Alamy; **p38** Courtesy of the Holocaust Memorial Day Trust, www.hmd.org.uk; **p39** *t* akg-images, *b* © David Sutherland/Corbis; **p40** U.S. Holocaust Memorial Museum *The views or opinions expressed in this book, and the context in which the images are used, do not necessarily reflect the views or policy of, nor imply approval or endorsement by, the United States Holocaust Memorial Museum*; **p41** Courtesy of The Wiener Library Photo Archive; **p44** *tl* U.S. Holocaust Memorial Museum, *tr* © Bettmann/Corbis, *cl* © Bettmann/Corbis, *cr* © Hulton-Deutsch Collection/Corbis, *bl* akg-images, *br* Courtesy of The Wiener Library Photo Archive; **p45** *tl* akg-images, *tr* U.S. Holocaust Memorial Museum, *cl* © Corbis, *cr* © Germany Images David Crossland/Alamy, *b* © Corbis; **p47** *tl* Deutsches Historisches Museum, Berlin, *tr* © mark saunders/Alamy, *bl* © Corbis, *br* © Frank Leonhardt/dpa/Corbis; **p48** © Bettmann/Corbis; **p50** *tl* © Trinity Mirror/Mirrorpi /Alamy, *tr* U.S. Holocaust Memorial Museum, *cl* U.S. Holocaust Memorial Museum, *cr* U.S. Holocaust Memorial Museum *b* U.S. Holocaust Memorial Museum; **p51** Courtesy of the Holocaust Memorial Day Trust, www.hmd.org.uk; **p52** *tl* Rex Features, *tr* TREVOR SAMSON/AFP/Getty Images, *bl* CARMEN TAYLOR/AP/Press Association Images, *br* © Jerry Lampen/Reuters/Corbis; **p53** *t* © Owen Franken/Corbis, *b* Stephen Ferry/Getty Images; **p54** © RIA Novosti/Alamy; **p55** Walter Sanders/Time Life Pictures/Getty Images; **p56** © Bettmann/Corbis; **p57** *t* © Bettmann/Corbis, *b* © Photos 12/Alamy; **p58** The Ronald Reagan Presidential Library; **p60** DISNEY/RGA; **p61** © Trinity Mirror/Mirrorpix/Alamy; **p62** © David Copeman/Alamy; **p64** *t* © reportage/Alamy, *b* © Martin Melaugh/CAIN (cain.ulster.ac.uk); **p67** *t* © Mary Evans Picture Library/Alamy; *b* Hulton Archive/Getty Images; **p70** *t* © National Museums Northern Ireland 2009, Collection Ulster Museum, Belfast/*Photograph reproduced courtesy the Trustees of National Museums Northern Ireland*, *b* Hulton Archive/Getty Images; **p72** *tl* © Hulton-Deutsch Collection/Corbis, *tr* © Corbis, *bl* Time Life Pictures/Mansell/Time Life Pictures/Getty Images, *br* © Bettmann/Corbis; **p73** *t* Hulton Archive/Getty Images, *b* National Museum of Ireland; **p74** ©Sean Sexton Collection/Corbis; **p78** *tr* © Adams Picture Library t/a apl/Alamy, *l* © Vincent MacNamara/Alamy, *ct* © JoeFoxDublin/Alamy, *cb* © Barry Mason/Alamy, **p81** *t* Sean Sexton/Getty Images, *b* Topical Press Agency/Getty Images; **p82** © Bettmann/Corbis; **p85** *t* Central Press/Getty Images, *c* Bert Hardy/Picture Post/Getty Images, *b* Paul Schwartzman, Camera Press London; **p86** © isifa Image Service s.r.o./Alamy; **p87** *t* Keystone/Hulton Archive/Getty Images, *b* © Bettmann/Corbis; **p88** *t* Ian Showell/Keystone/Getty Images, *b* Bentley Archive/Popperfoto/Getty Images; **p89** *t* Bentley Archive/ Popperfoto/Getty Images, *b* James Jackson/Evening Standard/Getty Images